The Kid From Kansas

Robert F Paden

Published by The Plowman, 2022.

THE KID FROM KANSAS

First edition. August 19, 2022.

Copyright © 2022 Robert F Paden.

ISBN: 979-8223563419

Written by Robert F Paden.

Dedication

This book is about America. The America that I love. My DNA is in this book. My parents and grandparents were pioneers. It is a tribute to them. My blood came from them, but the formation of a nation was also the formation of the character of those who inhabited that nation. We sang in school, *America, America, God shed his grace on thee. And crown thy good with brotherhood, from sea to shining sea!* Nathan Hale was one of my heroes. He said, "I regret that I have but one life to give to my country!" Abraham Lincoln was my favorite president. He said, "No one should be a slave, except those who want to be slaves and those who want others to be slaves." My father was a man of principles and he taught us those principles. Though he never talked much about God, he did instill in us a fear, an awe and a respect for "Almighty God". This story is a story of people who had values. They were willing to work hard, and even suffer, even die for those values. Mistakes? Yes! But in the middle of all that, forging personal identities and a national identity that weathered the Great Depression, hardships, even a World War. This is the story of the making of a young man, the making of a nation. I dedicate this book to all of them.

CHAPTER ONE
The Great Depression

THE LITTLE HOUSE ON THE HILL

The little frame house on a windswept hill in western Kansas didn't offer much protection from either the cold or the heat, but most people were living under pretty hard circumstances in those days. At another time or place it might have been called a shack, but it was not unusual for then and there. Back then, they didn't insulate houses like they do now. Many of the houses had been built "in a hurry" when they had good years and the wheat was a good price. But now times were really hard and they were thankful to have a house. In the winter the cold crept right through the walls and the snow came through the cracks. But now it was summer and that tremendous heat, and the wind. Would it never stop blowing? Everything was dry, and the dust so heavy and thick you could hardly breathe. They hadn't had a crop in two years. They had been forced to sell all the machinery and the horses; those beautiful horses! Dad was working at the blacksmith shop in town. He was an enterprising and versatile guy. Thank God they were able to keep the little Chevrolet roadster, two cows and an old sow pig, the only reminders of more prosperous times now past.

The heat was stifling! The old dug-outs that the first settlers lived in when they came to Kansas (including granddad and grandma) would have been more comfortable. The dugout was a practical refuge for the early settlers. The hills and breaks of that area lent themselves to such a dwelling. They were usually just one big room, half of it dug in to the steep bank and the other half made of 12" squares of sod laid like bricks. They were dark and small but cool in summer and warm in winter.

Those "homestead" days were long gone and progress and prosperity had visited western Kansas. These Kansas hills and plains seemed perfect for wheat and land prices were going up and up. Prosperity came and everything was moving fast. The houses were built fast; properties were bought and sold fast and at every sale a good profit was made. There seemed to be no end to the good times! These were the Flapper days. Some of the older men were skeptical about breaking up so much of the native "bunch grass" as they called it or "buffalo grass". In the twenties everyone was optimistic and no one had foreseen what was going to happen. When the stock markets fell in 'twenty nine', many people were still optimistic; After all, Wall Street is a long way from western Kansas! But then came the droughts and one right after another! One year they had a half of a crop and were hopeful, till the grasshoppers came. Could it be possible that God is punishing us? In clouds they came! Nobody had ever seen anything like it. You could see a cloud of grasshoppers coming from miles away. And the sound of their wings was like a weird wind! It would make your skin crawl. People devised everything they could think of to combat them. Kansas farmers were not ones to give up that easily. They tried a poison that looked like chewing tobacco and it did kill the hoppers, but they were so many that it didn't seem to make any difference. Then somebody came up with an idea that worked pretty well, at least for the few farmers that had a "hay buck rake". They tied a canvas to the back board of the buck rake and a trough of kerosene below it the width of the rake. The rakes were like a huge wooden pitch fork with a back and sides. They were pushed by two horses or a tractor or later a revised old truck turned around backwards. The buck rakes were made to pick up the hay from the wind rows. The grasshoppers would fly up when the rake teeth disturbed them and bounce off the canvas into the kerosene below the canvas. This killed a lot of grasshoppers but it still seemed for every hopper that was killed a thousand more came! The hoppers devoured everything! The crops, the tree leaves, the grass! Everything was left bare!

The hot winds came leaving nothing on those hills. Only in the little draws (small valleys) was there any grass left. It was a good thing they only had two cows and a pig to find feed for. But God in his mercy provided for them the milk and meat by the animals they still had and wood for cooking and heat in winter. Candles were devised from tallow (fat) and string. Everything else had been sold to pay off the debt. Even the truck, it was Dad's pride and joy. Like many other young guys at that time he had replaced the muffler and exhaust pipe with a long well casing. It had a ring to it that you could hear from miles away, especially when the truck was pulling a load. Each truck had a distinct sound and hearing a truck even miles away, people would say, "there goes Leo's truck or so and so's truck!

When they bought all these things it seemed like the thing to do, even though they went into debt to do it. Everything was going so well. They had almost a full line of machinery and horses, There was plenty of work for the truck and farming prospects were good, In their first years of marriage everything seemed to be going from good to better. They and several other newly married couples had such good times together. They all had good cars, nearly new too. They used to race down the dirt roads. What a carefree time it seemed to be!

Even at that they were more conservative than some of the others who plunged very deeply into debt. The banks were very lenient then and even anxious to loan money. And those that went into debt to buy things could sell out later and have money left over because everything was going up in value! Many people were buying and selling property just to speculate on the added value. But that was in the twenties. Then after the stock market crashed things started changing. Money got hard to get and jobs started getting scarce. After two years with no crops the banks started foreclosing on many people, Mom and Dad decided to sell out before the bank foreclosed on them. They were able to almost pay everything off, but they now had no machinery to farm with and no truck or horses to work with. Dad got a job in John Bronicle's big black smith shop and they were able to pay off the rest of the debt, but times were really getting hard now. It was the year 1934. It turned out to be the hottest year on record in western Kansas. They were in the middle of what was later called the Great Dust Bowl. Clouds of dust rose up in the sky so high that they were seen back as far as Indiana, more than 700 miles away, and finally in Washington DC!

They now had two little boys. Willis was three and a half years old, Mervyn was a year and a half and Mom was pregnant with what turned out to be another boy. Doctor Stephenson attended his patients in their houses as almost all doctors did back then. There was a small hospital in Norton, but that was many miles away and they only took care of the most severe cases. So Doc was notified that the time was getting close, so to be ready for Dad's roadster to come roaring up to his house! There were few telephones.

Meanwhile, summer wore on, and wear it did as the heat was stifling and the air so full of dust it was hard to breathe. Surely much of Mom's later problem with breathing was caused or worsened from living through that dust. She said that even with all the windows and doors shut as tight as they could be, the dust would come filtering in. It would settle a quarter inch thick on the backs of the chairs! Dad said that one afternoon he came home from work and the dust was so thick in the air that he couldn't even see the road. He could barely make out the thermometer on the radiator cap! He had to open the door and watch the ruts in the road to guide his way home. He said, "I really thought the end of the world had come! The sun was just a ball of fire in the sky!" The car engine was never the same after that.

So on August second 1934 Robert Fredric chose to come out into the world in that little frame house full of dust on a windswept hill. It was the hottest day of the hottest year on record in western Kansas. My Mom was five foot two and weighed about ninety five pounds but she had big babies. I was the smallest at eight and a half pounds. There were no nice facilities for the birth, only Doctor Stephenson and his bag in this little frame house that let in dirt through every small crack. That was the extent of the "medical team and delivery room". But Doc knew what he was doing and could do a lot with very little, like most country doctors in those days.

And grit, people had to have grit to survive those hard times. Those Kansas farmers and their wives in those parts had a lot of build in grit. Descendants of people who came to America from Europe to escape the tyranny of legalism, religious hypocrisy and the class system. Many were English, German and Scottish or "Scotch-Irish as they called themselves.. But this liberty that they looked for had a price, and they were willing to pay that price. That was part of my heritage. If you don't know what grit is, it's stay with it till it's done! You don't give up your goals when the going gets hard! You keep pressing on in spite of obstacles. Most people had a strong belief in God and that we are all ultimately responsible before God for our own actions. God's mercy was known, but the general understanding of the grace of God was that "God helps those who help themselves". Work hard and pay your own bills was a way of life and became, (perhaps even more through the struggles of the depression) their righteousness and almost their "religion". Though most folks perhaps weren't reading the Bible that much, they had a fear of God and a pretty high standard of righteousness.

CHAPTER TWO.
Looking For Work

When I was very small our parents took us to the State of Washington. Grandpa and Grandma Paden had settled in the eastern part of the state in the valley running between Spokane on the north and Colfax on the south. That valley has very deep rich soil and the terrain is mostly "sugar loaf hills" on each side. They plant those hills, even the steep slopes to wheat, not the hard red winter wheat of the plains but soft "cake flour" wheat. The drought of the Great Plains had not struck here and the wheat crop was good. Dad, Uncle Charles and Grandpa all got jobs as "thresher men" (threshing machine operators) since they were all experienced operators. Before he left Kansas, Grandpa had three very large threshing machines. He and my dad and uncle Charles each operated one. That was when Kansas with its good wheat crops was prosperous. Grandpa was an easy going guy and didn't insist that the farmers paid him right away when he threshed for them. I suppose he would have been a wealthy man had he collected all that was owed to him and sold his machines for a good price, neither of which was he able to do. The stock market fell, the droughts came and everything changed for almost everyone. So he parked the machines and the huge steam engines that pulled them and moved to eastern Washington State. I remember that two of the steam engines were parked on Grandpa Bull's farm. (My Grandmother's father) We boys would climb all over them when we visited Grandpa and Grandma Bull.

In Washington at that time they were already using combines, (the name comes from *combination* header and thresher) of a type especially adapted to the side hills. They were large machines and had a very large "bull wheel" (a wide ground power wheel to run the machine) and a leveling device that required another man to just keep the separating part of the machine on level. The machine was pulled by two very large powerful horses on the steering tongue and ahead of them twenty mules on a long chain. Mules are more agile than horses and on a turn the lead mule had to swing way out wide so that they would keep pulling the machine straight ahead and as the chain swung back the other mules had to jump over the chain to the outside and then jump back after they made the corner. The driver, the thresher man and the man who kept the machine on level all had to work closely together. Not only that but the horses and mules had to obey and sense the direction in which they had to pull. A man called a "sacker" worked high on a platform near the rear of the machine. The grain came up an elevator and poured out in little spouts on which were hooked empty sacks, and as each sack filled, the "sacker" tied it and slid it down a chute to a large basket then dumped them into piles in the field to later be picked up in wagons. These machines were forerunners of the huge self-propelled self-leveling combines that are used in that area today.

My Grandpa Paden was then janitor of a school. He and Grandma Paden lived in the school and that is where our family stayed. While Dad and Grandpa and Uncle Charles each worked as thresher men, my brothers and I stayed in the school since it was too dangerous for little boys to be around that machinery. The school, of course, was on summer vacation and we had lots of fun running around the halls of the school house. Once Merv fell into a deep concrete window well on his head, but he survived; and Willis got shut in a glass bookcase but also survived, although everyone was frantically looking for him for a while.

After wheat harvest we went down to Oregon where our folks planned to pick fruit. However, after the first day, they decided it wasn't worth it because they couldn't make much money and all the harvesters were bunched up at night in a make shift tent made of canvas tarps hanging on ropes. There was absolutely no privacy for the men and women and I think there were some things going on at night that Mom did not want her little boys to know about.

So we traveled on down the road toward Kansas. Along the way, we would stop in a cabin camps at night. They were forerunners of modern motels and consisted of little wooden cabins in a kind of park with picnic tables under the trees for eating. One evening it was just about dark and we had already eaten. We boys were using up the last bit of light to play. Another family had all girls and Merv was trying to impress them with his abilities. He got so enthused about his own prowess that he said, "I can jump off the end of a picnic table and flip clear over and land on my feet!" "Okay, let's see you do it" challenged one of the girls. You bet! said Merv, though he had never before done anything of the kind. Carried away with his own words, he jumped up on the table, ran the full length of it and did a perfect flip and landed on his feet! But no one was more surprised than Merv and his eyes were as big as saucers! I don't remember if the girls were impressed, but I sure was! He didn't push his luck and try it again, though.

When we arrived at Greeley Colorado, we stayed for a time. It was potato harvest time and Dad got a job "bucking spuds", which required a man to be strong and fast! Working alone, he would start the truck down the rows and the ditches between the rows would guide the truck. In first gear, the truck would creep along without a driver while he loaded the sacks of "spuds" on the truck. You had to keep up with the truck and not miss any sacks! At the end of the rows, you stop the truck, finish loading all the sacks and turn the truck around to start back!

After spud harvest he got a job remodeling and adding on to a house. Thanks to Dad's ability in many areas, including carpentry, our family would keep eating well and the folks possibly were able to put away something to help get started again on the farm.

Willis was in the first or second grade and went to school while we were there but kind of got started on the wrong foot. The teacher's name was Miss Gross and he misunderstood and called her Miss Grouch! It didn't help that she was kind of grouchy and she didn't appreciate him calling her that so her attitude toward him was not at all good! As I remember, he didn't like school there very well

CHAPTER THREE
Hard Times/Good Times

THE "120"

We called the farms by the number of acres each farm had. The "120" had 120 acres. We moved to the "120" sometime before my memory started to function probably before the Washington trip. Granddad Goldsmith had managed to give each one of his three daughters a farm. They were small farms for that area and ours was in the "breaks" (small valleys and hills) but it was a precious new start for the young couples. And now that the rains had come again, each couple made good use of the gift.

Granddad was a good business man and a shrewd trader. He had managed to stay out of debt and had a fair amount of capital in animals and machinery at the beginning of the depression. So he traded many different things including land which was very cheap then, till he had gotten a farm for each one of his daughters. He once said, "I'd trade for a wagon track if there was a dollar in it!" He also had a dairy farm of purebred Jerseys. He bottled his own milk and sold it delivered to the doorsteps in the town of Edmond in glass bottles, both pints and quarts, (no pasteurizing back then). I remember one time we boys were trusted with delivering some of the milk. It was a great adventure for me. We had to cross the highway that passed by his farm to go to town (about ½ mile). Dad taught us to never run across the road, in that manner teaching us to have a healthy fear of traffic.

Our farm was about 3 miles from town. It had a creek which flowed its full length with springs breaking out of the hillsides along the way. So these small valleys or "draws" as we called them took up most of the farm and it only had a small amount of higher land for planting crops. It wasn't the best farm land around, but it served as pasture for the animals and it sure was a paradise for us three boys with woods and creeks and ponds. Dad had built a basement house with the idea to build a house above later. It was the most practical and cheapest way to start, taking perhaps from the idea of the old dugout house, but with cement walls to support a house above later.

For us boys that farm was the best place in the world to spend our childhood. We spent hours climbing the trees and crawling around up there on top of the wild grape vines that grew in abundance. The vines made practically a floor about six or eight feet off the ground. We had a dog that was always with us wherever we wandered among the trees and hills. His name was Pyge. When Mom wanted us to come to the house, she would call pyge and he would perk up his ears and start towards the house. We knew Mom was calling and soon we too would be able to hear her voice. He was probably a better guardian than most! He was a really smart dog. Unfortunately later on, he got left at a camp site on a trip, and though we went back and searched diligently for him, he never showed up. We were so sad to lose him!

Times were better now, our cows had multiplied and the pigs as well so there was milk every day and animals to butcher for meat. From somewhere we got a billy goat once. Dad would get so mad at that goat! The first thing in the morning when the goat could hear us start moving around inside the house, he would jump up on the low flat roof. Dad would yell at him to get off and he would just run around up there all the more till finally one of us would go to the door to run him off. When he heard the door open, he would jump off and come around to be petted! If a neighbor would come in a car or pickup he would climb on top of it before anyone could stop him! I don't remember what happened to "Billy" but he disappeared!

The farm wasn't big enough to produce more than feed for the livestock and without any cash crops Dad had to work out. He got a job at Walt Hunter's big farms in the summer. Walt was one that made it through the depression years in good shape financially. So when the rains came again, he began to plow and plant. He bought two new big Case tractors and during the summer ran them day and night with men working up to 12 hour shifts. During wheat harvest the tractors would pull combines all day then for the night shift they were hooked up to one-way plows to plow up the ground behind the combines. Dad decided to try working a double shift, (day and night!) since the plowing was pretty easy work!? You just put the front wheel in the furrow and the tractor would guide itself around and around the field. All you had to do was wake up in time to turn the corners! That way you could catch a little sleep on each round and so be able to work day and night! But one night he woke up with the tractor teetering on the edge of a deep gulch that would have turned the tractor over and surely killed him! That was the last night shift he worked that summer!

TO GET THROUGH THE WINTER

At the end of the summer and after the wheat was planted in the fall, Walt Hunter's operations came to a stop. Dad had done well that summer and had forty some dollars left over to get through the winter with; two crisp twenty dollar bills and some smaller bills. In the winter time in western Kansas there was very little outside work to be had, but Mom and Dad felt they could make it through the winter easy enough on forty dollars. So Dad and Mom and we three boys all went to the county fair in Norton to celebrate on Labor Day. Though I was still very young, I remember that particular day so very clearly, not for the fair and not for the animals nor the rides, (I don't think we took any rides) but for the anguish that my folks went through when Dad discovered that someone had picked his pocket and stolen the two twenty dollar bills! Winter was coming on and we had no money! There was no such thing as welfare in those days. President Roosevelt had started some work programs for men without work but Dad did not at all like depending on the government for help.

But God showed his mercy on us and Dad was resourceful in times of difficulty. Dad and Mom decided that on Tuesday morning (after Labor Day) he would go to our little town of Edmond and asked

Shag Smith, the owner of one of the two general stores for credit to somehow get through the winter. He would buy just the bare essentials like flour, sugar, salt and bullets. Yes bullets! Because hunting would be a very serious business.

However, when he got to the door of Smith's General Store, Shag was in the process of turning down another man who had just asked him for credit. Dad turned to leave, but then he thought, what will the kids eat? I've got to ask him for their sake! So he mustered his courage and went in. He explained what had happened, how he had lost his summer's wages and told Shag. I just want to buy the essentials. And the minute I can get some work, you know I'll pay you every cent and with interest! Shag said, "No Leo, you won't pay me any interest! I trust you and know you're a man of your word! You can buy whutever yu need, and all winter long! When comes spring and you have a good job, you come in on your own time and we'll settle up, but meanwhile don't you worry! You just git what yu need!"

So included in the purchases that day was a box of bullets, "22 longs". The "22 long rifle" would be unnecessarily expensive and the "22 shorts" were not trustworthy enough to shoot straight for much distance. This was important business. The game would be principally cottontail rabbits for good fresh meat on the table.

So important was this hunting business that after much discussion Dad and Mom decided to trade his old rifle and Mom's washing machine for a better rifle! Mom had two washers. One had a half-moon tub with a handle in the middle that sloshed the water back and forth as you moved the handle. It wasn't easy to wash clothes with it but the other folks had nothing and were glad to get it, and for Dad a good rifle was very important. Dad said, "I figured I had to make and average of two rabbits for every three shells and I beat my average!"

CHRISTMAS WITHOUT MONEY

Christmas was not very spiritual. I don't remember Christ's name being mentioned, but it was a special family time. I remember Dad starting in early December saying just every once in a while, "Christmas is coming!" We would all get so excited! A good part of the joy of Christmas was just waiting for it! But this year there was no money for special gifts and the folks were very concerned that it might not be a happy time. So Dad in secret made each of us three boys a little wooden wheelbarrow with a wooden wheel and painted them pretty red! They felt they could only buy something useful so they bought each of us a pair of bib overalls! But to me it was a very special time because I felt so much love from our parents. So now, more than seventy years later I remember with fondness that special Christmas without money! Later Dad made us a wooden sled with a steel rod under each side for a runner. What fun we had sliding down those slopes in the snow!

Dad didn't have a tractor but was able to get an old truck which he planned to make into a tractor to work the small amount of farm land we had. He worked and worked so hard making that old truck into a tractor, shortening the frame, putting on a hitch and fixing the steering. Then the old thing wouldn't ever start. I remember how Dad cranked and cranked and tried this and tried that to make it start. But evidently the old engine was pretty well worn out. The "hard times" of the great depression lasted longer in Kansas than some other places. Finally he was able to get an old Wallace tractor. It was huge and heavy but didn't have much power. At least he was able to put in a crop with it.

Though they were "hard times" economically, our folks had a lot of fun and I can never remember going hungry or feeling deprived or depressed. It was a good life. Sometimes Dad would grab Mom up in his arms and run around the house with her screaming, "Put me down, put me down!" But we all knew it was in fun and we would run around behind them laughing and enjoying the whole affair! The dust bowl was just a memory and our folks "made do" with what we had. They raised chickens and turkeys, pigs and cattle. We boys helped herd the turkeys because they don't have a sense of where home is and will just wander off and get lost! Earlier on (this was before my memory was functioning) Mom was herding turkeys and my brother Merv saved my life. I was just beginning to walk and somehow managed to get over the side of the horse tank and fell in the water head first. They had never cut my hair and it was really long. I looked like a girl! Maybe Mom wanted a girl very badly. I guess I really disappointed her because I wasn't much of a girl! Anyway, Merv grabbed my long hair and held my head out of the water and I suppose we were both were screaming bloody murder. Mom came running (about 200 yards) while Merv held my head up and was able to save me.

Sometimes we ate whole wheat for breakfast. They would wash it and wash it, then soak it all night and cook it in the morning for our cereal. With fresh cream from the cows and sugar on it; boy, was that good! And it really stuck with you all morning too! We also used corn flour for bread. Dad would grind it with the finest sieve on the grinder to make corn bread.

In the winter time, the folks loved to play cards with their friends. It was always a special occasion. How well I remember the excitement of getting ready and going to those parties! We would play with the other youngsters until we got tired and then crawl behind the stove or in some corner on the floor and go to sleep. I think the thing that made me like it so well was that the folks seemed to have such a good time. I remember Dad laughing. He loved a good joke and loved to laugh and enjoy good company. Those were clean and healthy parties. I don't know if they drank anything other than coffee, if they did it wasn't very much. There were no hangovers, no fights and though we got home late and Dad would carry me in, the next morning life and work went on as usual.

CHAPTER FOUR
Going To Edmond

Edmond was our town. We were only about three miles from town but the road was not a very good one. Half of it was mostly clay, so in wet weather it was almost impossible to drive on it and in dry weather it always had ruts. So it wasn't so easy to just "run into town". Sometimes the battery was down on the car and we had to push it down the hill by the house to start it. In front of the house the hill dropped sharply to the bottom of the draw and sometimes that served really well for starting the car. Behind the house the lane was a steady climb up to the road. Sometimes when Mom was by herself, she wouldn't manage to get the car started before we got to the bottom. She would cry a little and of course we would have to wait till Dad got home to start the car. The trip to Edmond would have to be postponed for the day. But even after getting the car started we might get stuck before we even got out on the road if it was muddy. The road went past Boatman's house and then curved to the right to cross the next draw. "Nigger" Bob's little house set back off the road in the bottom of the draw. He would sometimes ride with us for a ways and always was very respectful. He rode out on the running board and would have never thought of getting into the car or the truck. People liked him and spoke well of him but no one would have inquired about his life. He had a family and a small farm. They raised watermelons, cantaloupes and pigs for a living.

Why did he choose to come to western Kansas and live? Nobody seemed to know or bother to ask him. But he was free and there was a mutual respect, even though they called him "Nigger Bob" and he rode on the outside instead of inside. He even called himself Nigger Bob. It never occurred to us boys to ask questions either. That's just the way things were at that point in time.

After passing Bob's house, the road wound up the next hill and soon joined the County road that was wider and sometimes it was even freshly graveled. Soon we came to the "Little Salmon" Valley in which was nestled the little town of Edmond. As we came to the edge of the hill that overlooked the valley we could see the river right at the bottom of the hill and the railroad tracks that passed through town and curved around following the bend of the Little Salmon up to the town of Lenora, ten miles to the north. It was a short railroad that started in Densmore, eight miles to the south and ended in Lenora and its only train was a very short combination freight, mail and passenger with two or three cars and a small engine. The folks around there called it the "Jitterbug". It made one or two trips to Lenora most days.

The hill was very steep which descended down to the river. There was a narrow one-lane bridge that crossed the Little Salmon. Just before we crossed the Salmon, we passed the Old Mill. I don't remember seeing it work, but I do remember the old paddle mill wheel that turned by the force of the river water and powered the mill.

The bridge had a floor of cross planks and over that two rows of planks for the wheels of the cars and trucks. I always held my breath when we went down that steep hill for fear we would miss the bridge and fall in the river or at least fall off the planks! And since the road was cut through a pure clay bank, it seemed like we might slide off one side or the other. It was always a relief to get onto the bridge straight!

Coming into Edmond, we went past John Bronicle's big blacksmith and machine shop. When we crossed the railroad tracks there were only a few blocks of houses before we came to Main Street and the middle of town. In my memory I'd guess the town was only about six blocks wide. Main Street boasted board sidewalks for a couple of blocks in the center, beyond that they were just dirt. Shag Smith's general store was on one side of the street and the IGA grocery store on the other side. Near the end of town going west was the filling station and garage. The gas pumps had a big long handle to pump the gas up into the a glass container at the top of the "pump". The gallons were marked on the side of the glass and the attendant pumped up the amount ordered, then took down the hose and drained it into your car.

Up the hill on the north side was the school and going east going out of town was the dance hall. Saturday night was dance night and Dad and Mom went to the dance at least a couple of times that I remember. Of course we went with them. Baby sitting was unknown. I don't know what the "big" people did but the young boys would sit on one side of the hall and the girls on the other. The boys would try to get up nerve enough to ask a girl to dance. Then they would go out on the dance floor and to the tune of the fiddle over in the far corner, they would move around with the girl and pretend they knew how to dance!

There were several other stores along Main Street and most of them still had a hitching rails in front to accommodate the folks that came to town on horseback or with a wagon, which was still quite common.

I don't remember there being a church building, but occasionally they held special meetings in a tent and we would go. We usually got there late and if they were praying Dad would hush us up and we would all reverently bow our heads and close our eyes until they finished praying. At least we learned reverence before the things of God. I don't remember anything about what was preached though.

SHAG SMITH'S GENERAL STORE

It was kind of dark in there and on a cloudy day there was usually one or two kerosene lanterns lit and hanging from the ceiling. There was a potbellied stove right in the middle of the store and in the winter the farmers sat around the stove on old chairs or nail kegs and swapped yarns. The spittoon was an interesting part of the furnishings because many of the men chewed tobacco. Most could spit a stream of tobacco juice for several yards into or near the spittoon without hardly missing a word in the "yarn" they were spinning.

The store and the merchandise were very interesting to me because Shag sold just about everything, hardware, groceries, feed for chickens and livestock, veterinarian supplies, dishes and silverware, tools, harness for horses and just about anything else you might need on the farm. Many things came shipped in barrels and kegs so they were in abundance around the big room. Sacked feed was stacked in separate piles according the type. Some stacks went all the way to the ceiling which was at least ten feet high. Shag, the proprietor was an amiable sort and well able to hold his own in any conversation. I would just watch and listen. But I loved it. The store had a special smell. The ground feed, bread, oil, harness leather, tobacco juice and some other unidentified smells all mixed together made a very particular smell that identified that place in that time. I could have walked in there blindfolded and known for sure that I was in Shag Smith's General Store!

Edmond was small; probably less than a1000 people lived there, but it was our town. Saturday was "trading" day. That word came from the old bartering system where farmers took their produce to town and virtually traded it for the merchandise they needed. We didn't do that, but it wasn't far from it. We took cream and eggs to the railroad station where they would be shipped to Lenora or maybe all the way to the county seat which was Norton, 20 some miles to the north. The cream would be tested for grade and weighed and the eggs checked for cracks and size then they would give Dad a receipt and every fifteen days or so he would get a check for the amount. Times were still not easy and the money didn't go very far, but I can never remember going hungry and I don't remember the folks complaining'

THE BLACKSMITH SHOP

I think Dad worked several times at John Bronicle's big shop in the winter. Sometimes I got to go into the shop and look around. Dad wouldn't let me run around loose in the shop but I loved to watch the machines work. The shop was powered with a big engine outside that ran a main overhead shaft which extended the full length of the shop. This shaft had all different sizes of pulleys along its length for the different machines, and a loose belt that hung from the each pulley down next to a machine. The size of the pulley determined the speed of the machine. When one of the men wanted to use a machine he would use a stick to flip that particular belt onto the machine's pulley and that machine would suddenly be turning full speed. If it was a larger machine, the big engine outside would let out a puff of smoke, the governor would open up and you would hear the engine "talk louder" as it would "lean into" the extra load it had to pull.

As well as many things those days, the shop was all purpose. They did all types of mechanic and "blacksmith" work which was any and all kinds of iron work including shoeing horses. Welding and shaping irons was done by heating the irons in the coal burning forge. What you wanted to do with the iron determined the how hot you would heat it in the big forge. In general it was red hot for bending and white hot for welding. They used number two hard coal in the forge which would fan it into a tremendously hot fire. The hot irons would be bent into the shape desired or to be "welded" together, which was done by pounding two white hot irons together until they were fused into one piece. That shop and the men who worked there fixed or manufactured just about anything the farmers needed around there. John was also an expert lathe machinist, remaking or rebuilding parts for repairs and even building machines. "Yankee ingenuity" is not just a saying. America was literally forged and built by men and women who lived by "if there is a will, there is a way!" and "God helps those who help themselves!" Most of the progress in agricultural machinery and technology for many years was accomplished on the farms and in the shops of rural America.

SURGERY IN 1939

Dad was fixing a tractor one cold winter day outside the shop. He was doing some work underneath the tractor when a loose wheel lug, a wedge shaped piece of steel with a sharp edge weighing about two pounds, fell off the top of the wheel with the sharp side down onto his wrist. It cut both tendons through. He came home that night with it bandaged up but it hurt so bad that Mom opened the bandage and realized that the tendons were cut in two. I can still remember the smell of blood mixed with the kerosene they had put on the wound for disinfectant. (There is none better.) There were no emergency rooms in those days. He would have to wait. It was Saturday night.

They decided that he would drive to Norton on Monday morning and that I would accompany him. I was just five and not yet in school. Lenora was closer and Doc Stephenson was there, but though Dad always called Doctor Stykens in Norton a "horse doctor" because he was so rough, he knew that for surgical skill there was no equal in all of Norton County. So they decided that he should go there and that I would accompany him.

We started out real early when it was still dark and got to Norton about eight-thirty. It was a cold day and after the twenty three mile trip it was good to get into the warm doctor's office. I don't know how Dad managed to drive all the way with one hand and the other one hurting so badly. When we went in to the waiting room no one else was there and Doc took Dad right in. He took a good look at Dad's wrist and saw that the tendons had drawn back up into his arm! He just said, "Humph!", took a pair of pincers and started pushing them up under his skin. Dad yelled like all get out and Doc stopped, looked him in the eye and said, "<u>What's</u> the matter? <u>Can't you take it</u>?" It turned out that he didn't have any sedative of any kind on hand, but he hadn't said that. He knew a lot about human nature though, and knew his men. He had to do something and do it right away. Any kind of anesthetic may have been days away in which time the chance of repairing that hand could be lost. This was going to hurt and hurt really bad, but it might be the difference between Dad having a useful hand or being a cripple for the rest of his life.

The doctors had another out in those days if they judged the patient to be of hardy stock. It's called adrenaline. If your veins are full of adrenaline you don't feel pain nearly so badly and one thing that will make the adrenaline rise is anger, so he purposely made Dad mad. His manhood had been challenged and he said, "Hell yes I can take it!" I don't remember if Doc had a nurse helping him or not but he quickly proceeded to do his job: reach up under the skin, stretch those tendons down and stitch them together. I don't know how he did it but it didn't take him long, and Dad just gritted his teeth and the sweat poured out of his brow, but he didn't yell again!

After Doc finished sewing up the skin, Dad paid him the few dollars he asked for and we went down to the restaurant. Dad ordered a stiff cup of coffee (it might have had a little something else laced into it). Then we drove the twenty some miles back home. Dad was still kind of mad, but you know what? The wound never infected and he never, for the rest of his life, ever had any problem with the use of that hand! But he still called Doc Stykens a horse doctor! The stitches were made of cat gut and in time rotted and fell out so there was no need to visit the doctor again!

MY FIRST DAY OF SCHOOL

I couldn't wait to start school. My two older brothers had been going to school now for several years and I was missing out. Between them and my Mom, who had been a school teacher when she was single, they read to me a lot and taught me some elementary reading. It was almost two miles to school and was a real adventure just to go there. We followed our creek down to where a spring came out of the side of the hill; from there the trail started up over the hill to Brook's valley. We went through the Brook's yard where Don and Todd Brooks joined us. Todd was Willis's age and Don was older. They kind of took up with me and when we went through the swamp, each would take one of my arms and literally carry me over the swamp. There were rocks and logs to step on but every once in a while somebody would slip and get their feet wet.

Maxine McKee was my first grade teacher and she was a good teacher, but the first day she didn't impress me at all. She started out with great patience to teach me the letters one at a time. I already knew that and it disappointed and bored me. When I got home I told Mom. I don't think I'll go to school anymore! Mom was very surprised because I had waited for the day I could go to school for so long. She said, "why?" I told her that it wouldn't do any good because obviously I knew more than the teacher!

Well, what was really obvious of course was my out sized estimation of myself. My Mom convinced me that I could probably still learn some things in school and my Dad said, "Young man, you <u>will</u> go to school tomorrow and from now on! Not another word from you about not going to school!"

But then I really learned to enjoy school and every part of it. Learning from books was to me like another adventure, discovering new words and later being able to read stories and take the treasures out of those books! I loved working with numbers too. It was like using building blocks to make something out of pieces. School meant learning Reading, Writing and arithmetic. That's what we went to school for and that's what we learned. It would have been a shame for a child to come out of the first grade without knowing how to read and write and work with numbers, (all basic of course)!

Silver Creek was the name of the school, named from the creek that ran down the steep gully behind the school. One day the teachers let all the students take time out to pick choke cherries that grew in abundance along the banks of the creek.

A State road ran right in front of the school. State roads were better than County roads and County roads were better than the township roads. They were "oiling" the road that year. It was a forerunner of the asphalt roads. They spread gravel very evenly and then with a tank truck filled with liquid asphalt and spigots on the back, they spread it slowly on the gravel until it filled up the cracks and formed an asphalt surface. We weren't supposed to walk on it for several days and since we had to cross the road to go home we put some rocks and boards down to get across.

Recess and noon hour were great too. That year someone had left a pile of gunny sacks from harvest and the older boys quickly came up with a great project of making rooms and halls by hanging the sacks on wires. What fun it was to crawl around in those halls and rooms during recess and noon hour!

One afternoon after school Willis and Todd got into a fight. I don't know who was winning but my loyalty was definitely with my brother. I grabbed Todd's nose and wrung it till it began to bleed! That was the end of that fight!

CHAPTER FIVE
The "320"

It was February and a cold cloudy day, but that didn't matter. We were so excited. The truck was loaded to the limit to the top of the stock racks. Neighbors and friends had helped. I remember one guy, kind of fat, who wanted to show how strong he was. They had to move the piano out of the basement house up the narrow stairs and load it on the truck. He claimed he could lift the whole piano if he could just get a good hold on it. He had been drinking and Dad just laughed because he knew it was more bluster than anything else. In the end, he couldn't even handle one end of it and dropped it half way up the stairs! It was a big mess and something broke. One of the other guys had to climb over the piano to help him, but they managed to get it out and loaded. The kitchen stove was kind of heavy too, but not that bad. There were so many things to bundle up and put in boxes. They kept telling me to stay out of the way please! But I just had to be a part of all that was going on. I was six at the time.

I had not seen the 320 yet. I think Dad had taken Willis to help him get things ready on the new farm. Dad and Mom had talked a lot about it before they made the decision to make the trade with money "to boot". They had to go into debt to do it, but it was a good farm and would give us the opportunity to have both a cattle operation and raise a cash crop to sell on top of that. The 120 was just too small for a good farming operation. I loved those trees and creeks, valleys and hills of the "120", but they just couldn't make a living there and so after looking all around they found this chance to trade for a bigger and better farm. It was about half flat farm ground and the other half was hills and valleys covered with virgin Buffalo grass that had never been plowed. The cattle would have plenty to eat. I grew to love that land, though at first it seemed bare. There was not a tree on the place when we came. We soon planted trees all around the house though. 320 acres was also called a half section. It was one mile long and one half mile wide. A county road ran along the west side and the south end of the farm.

The house and barn were wood frame buildings and the house was really quite small. It didn't seem so small to us at the time, but we sure felt the cold the first night. Drafts of wind came in from everywhere. In the winter months Mom always read a chapter of a story to us each evening. It was a very special event, sitting around the fire and maybe on Dad's lap listening to the story. I don't remember the title of the book we read that spring, but I do remember that the family in the story lived in a ramshackle house that let in the cold on every side and had been built by a man named Fraiden, and they called the house Fraiden's Folly. We had bought the 320 from a man named Hayden so we dubbed our house Hayden's Folly! But Dad already had plans to make that house more livable and before summer was over, he had added a nice living room, a dining room, remodeled the two bedrooms and insulated the entire house. We never passed through another winter in the cold!

Our closest neighbors were the Keevers, about one third mile to the north. Their only son, Loren was about a grown man but still lived at home. He worked for Dad sometimes and he was a "good man", meaning a good reliable worker. Keevers had an old pick up, but Mr. Keever had never learned to drive very well. He would come to a corner and start yelling whoa whoa! And pull hard on the steering wheel, but that pickup just wouldn't slow down so he would skid around the corner at the same speed and about that time find the brake pedal and come to a skidding halt. Somehow he managed not to have an accident while we lived there though years later did have a grave accident that took the life of his wife.

Both farmsteads were infested with sparrows. We boys had a b.b. gun (air rifle) and would go out at night with a flashlight and hunt sparrows. Dad would give us a penny a sparrow and we earned several dollars hunting sparrows! After we began to decimate the sparrow population Mr. Keever said one day. I just don't know what has happened to all the sparrows! There used to be so many of them and now there are just a few! Dad just smiled because he wasn't sure Mr. Keever was in favor of killing the sparrows even though they had become a pestilence. Since the sparrows would fly back and forth from barn to barn, we, without realizing it, were taking down the sparrow population of both farms! We also got a penny for killing 100 flies! Between flies and sparrows, we felt like we were really in the money!

CHUB

One day Dad said, "When I was a kid I had a horse. She was half Shetland and half "Indian" (pinto mustang). She may be still alive. Both those breeds are noted for their longevity. Let's see now, she would be about twenty eight years old now!" So we went looking and, yes she was alive and for years had been "out to pasture". The man said, "I think she is still healthy enough". So Dad bought her back and what good times we had with that horse! She was larger than Shetland and smaller than Mustang and was a mighty ball of energy. She was always hard to catch up in the pasture. You had to go out with an offering of grain or hay and hide the bridle behind your back. If she caught sight of the bridle she would go running off with her tail in the air as if to say, phooey on you! But once you caught her up and wrapped a rein around her neck, she was docile enough. Except for a couple of habits she had, like laying down in the middle of a stream or pond of water. No matter how much you urged and kicked and shouted, she would just lie down and get wet along with her rider or riders. Then there was her love for racing and her determination never to lose a race. We would be riding along with other kids from the neighborhood with their horses. If we started to race or another horse bolted she would take off with all her might! She became a wild thing! You'd better hang on because she was going to win that race at all costs! She would get so mad at another horse if they got within biting distance and would reach over and bite the ear or neck of the horse that dared to come close to her without losing stride even a little bit. I don't ever remember her losing a race. She could outrun any horse in the neighborhood. Several of the neighbors' horses were quite a bit bigger than her, but that didn't daunt her even in the least. She was out to win every race! And that with all three of us on her sometimes.

Many sunny days we three boys passed in sublime peace and joy on old Chub. Willis always took the reins when we all three rode together, Merv in the middle and I in the back. We never used a saddle. We didn't even own one. Dad didn't want us to use a saddle for the danger of getting a foot caught in the stirrup and getting drug to death. Well this way we could fall off freely, which we often did. I especially since I was in the back and Chub was short coupled, my place was almost on the backside of her rump. How many times, Willis would kick her in the ribs and she would suddenly break into a full gallop. Where would I be left? On the ground! She would start off so suddenly that I would just do a full flip and land on my rump! Sometimes if I was lucky I would land on my feet, but that didn't happen very often.

ON THE PRAIRIES OF KANSAS

If we thought at first that those hills and draws were uninteresting because they were treeless, we were mistaken. The draws (small valleys) were fairly flat on the bottom and each side rose very quickly to the level above forming in many places small cliffs. These little short cliffs or "breaks" as they are called were full of life. They made a very convenient and easy place for small and middle size animals to dig their dens. Badgers were famous for making several dens with only one entrance which they used for "trap lines". Rabbits and other smaller animals would use them and Mr. Badger would come along and have his dinner quite easily. The one he used for home always had several exits so that a larger animal could not trap him. But there was one animal that Mr. Badger would not bother if he took up residence in one of his holes and that was Mr. Skunk. The porcupine was another animal that didn't worry too much about enemies.

Coyote dens were bigger and you would right away note that it had probably been used by coyotes. (We pronounced them cayoots.) A coyote is classified as a small wolf. They are about the size of an English Shepherd and in western Kansas they were always thin. They were at the same time a source of great admiration; our friends; and our enemies. Admiration because they were so intelligent, friends because we would have great fun howling with them on a moonlight night, and enemies because they stole and ate our chickens and would even lure a pup off occasionally. Lambs were also an easy prey for them. We could always tell when it was a coyote that killed a chicken because there would only be a ring of a few feathers left and right in the middle of the ring would be the gizzard picked clean. The coyotes would eat everything, all the feet, the head and most of the feathers. But there was one thing a coyote would not touch and that was the gizzard. So if we found a ring of a few feathers on the ground with a gizzard in the middle, picked clean, we knew a chicken had been killed by a coyote.

They would stealthily come up behind the barn just before sundown and catch an unwary chicken before it could even squawk! Coyotes are cunning animals. Two or more would chase a jack rabbit; but not side by side. A rabbit will always run in a wide circle, perhaps covering more than two miles. So the other coyote would wait in hiding and when his partner went by would relieve him. In that way they always out ran their prey!

We would hunt their dens constantly because the County paid a bounty of two dollars for each pelt, which were the two ears connected by a strip of skin in between. They were usually too stealthy for us to catch them. But we got pretty sharp at it too as we would smell each hole to see if they were in there. If we thought we smelled them, we would leave a cap of some piece of clothing off our backs and run for help to dig them out. The coyote would not venture past the smell of a human. I can remember of only once though that we were able to dig up a whole litter of pups.

Many times on moonlight nights we would go out in the yard and start howling in imitation of the coyotes. After a short time one would answer us off in some direction. We could imitate them close enough that they thought we were one of them! Soon another would answer over in another direction, then another then another. After a while we would have the whole countryside echoing with coyotes howling! What great fun that was!

WOLF

Sometimes when we found a large and empty den, we would enlarge it more to make a cave for us. This always had to be kept secret because Mom didn't want us to be crawling into a cave that might fall in on us. The thought of that didn't stop us much, so we would not say a word about our current cave that we were working on!

Our great helper in all this was our dog and constant companion, "Wolf" A big dog; he was half Collie and half Shepherd with the long hair of the Collie. He was a bit of a coward when by himself but when he was with us and we would encourage him, he would fight anything! I remember one time when the men were working on the road in front of the house. The large neighbor dog was there and Wolf wanted to run him off, but since he was afraid to face him, he faced our house with the other dog behind him and barked fiercely!

He would help us a great deal in digging out caves as we would get him all excited by saying, "Dig boy dig!" And dig he would with all his might as though his very life depended on it. In fact much of our digging was done that way!

Wolf was nearly grown when we got him but still a pup by nature. He took to us and we to him like only dogs and kids can do. Dad tried in vain to teach him to "heel" when driving cattle. The problem was that Wolf became our dog body and soul and he would look a Dad like, "What is it you want? I don't understand your language!" Now with us driving the cattle was a different story. Though he never learned to "heel" and drive them by himself, he would respond perfectly to our direct commands. But we never knew how to teach him either. In driving cows we would tell him "sic em" and he would charge after the cows. Then we would say, "Okay" or "That's enough!" and he would come back. So that's how we managed the cows. What we were doing was training the cows too. Just the sssss of sic em would put mortal fear into the cows and they would get into the corral or move on. They were ready to do anything so that the dog would not come after them.

We were never afraid of bulls or any danger as long as Wolf was with us, because even the bulls had a healthy respect for him. Our neighbors the Walters lived on the opposite corner of our section, about one and a half miles from our house. They also had a large bull and sometimes he would get out and come visit our bull. They would get into a fight and make the ground shake, they were so large. When they came together head to head, it was like two freight trains colliding. But Wolf would not let anything fight in our yard, roosters, cats or bulls! He would take after those bulls with fury and grab the nose of the neighbor's bull. That's about the only tender spot on a bull. This dog weighed forty or fifty pounds and he would hang on to the bull's nose and the bull would swing him around trying to get rid of him till his nose tore loose. By that time Mr. bull had forgotten all about fight and was wondering why he had ever come here. He would break back out of the corral like he broke in and start trotting for home, Wolf right behind him!

In my wanderings around the range I would occasionally spot a cotton tail rabbit. With Wolf's help I would soon catch and kill it. Then I would hunt up Dad, fixing fence or working on machinery and he would squat down while I held the hind feet of the rabbit and with his jackknife very soon skin and gut it and we would have rabbit for dinner!

One time we smelled a skunk inside a cave we'd been working on. Since Wolf could do anything, we sent him in to bring out Mr. Skunk. So at our urging in he went, grabbed the skunk and came backing out with the skunk in his mouth upside down. Well Mr. Skunk just did a curving act and squirted Wolf right in the nose with his special odor. Poor Wolf. He got so sick and I felt so sorry for him. He was sick for a week and smelled like skunk for a month. We knew better than to do that again!

A WILD TEAM OF HORSES

Dad had a team that he used for some of the farm work, like hauling hay or building fence. But they were both kind of a problem: the gelding because he was very skittish and the mare because she was just downright ornery! Because he didn't work them every day, they weren't very dependable. One day when he was fixing fence and had many yards of wire unrolled to later stretch up on the fence posts. Something scared the horses and they took off with the wagon loaded with tools, wire and posts. Before they had stopped they tangled up over one hundred yards of wire because one horse ran down one side of the wire and the other horse ran down the other side! They couldn't have done a better job of messing things up if they had planned it!

One day I was with Dad and we were coming back to the house in the wagon when something startled the horses and they took off running at a full gallop with the wagon bouncing along behind them. Dad said, "hang on! (I already was!) Our house was set back from the road a ways and there were two driveways, one on each side of the house in form of a "V". The yard behind the house was in kind of a square, bordered on each side by the house, the windmill, stock tank and corrals, the barn, and the chicken houses. Dad was heaving back on the reins for all his might when the horses with wagon bouncing along behind came into the yard at a full gallop. I thought they might run right into the barn. They were going way too fast to stop. The right rein broke and Dad hauled their heads around to the left. That was the only thing that turned them because by then they were like two senseless creatures, full of panic and blind. They ran around and around the yard, still at full gallop, the tail end of the wagon skidding around and hitting everything as it went by; the tank and corrals, the barn and the chicken houses. I was hanging on for dear life and wasn't about to jump off. After about the second round though I stopped being scared and kind of enjoyed the ride! I don't know how many rounds they made but after a while they ran out of steam and started slowing down until they finally stopped. Mom was so thankful that we weren't hurt. Dad just said, "dumb horses!" (Or maybe it was "damn!") Fortunately Dad was able to repair the damage.

WINTER MORNINGS

We had to get up early in the winter as well to get our chores done before going to school. We had to thaw out the pump so the windmill could keep the cows "in water". Dad told us not to stick our tongue on the pump because it would freeze our tongue and leave some skin on the pump. So each of us had to try it out once! Sure enough! It left some skin on the pump! Once was enough though!

Our school was almost two miles from the house by the road, but if we cut across the field it was about a mile and a half. We got permission from the neighbor to make a path through his wheat field if we would promise to stay on the path and not make it too wide! School started at nine and let out at four with an hour for lunch and a fifteen minute recess in the morning and afternoon. It was a one room building with a porch for coats, caps and overshoes. Grades one through eight were all housed in one big room. There was a row of desks down each side. The desks were connected by two runner boards to which each desk was bolted. The front of each desk was the back and seat for the next desk and each was wide enough for two small students to sit. In the middle of the room was a potbellied stove. Across the end of the room the floor was raised about two inches to form a "platform" where the teacher's desk was situated and the student or students who were reciting their lessons stood. From wall to wall behind the teacher's desk was the blackboard. There were several large windows along each of the side walls and between the windows hung kerosene lamps with a reflector behind each lamp. The building was also used for the community meetings. The yard of the school was quite large, about an acre, and in the back of the school yard was a shed for horses when students came on horseback. The name of this school was Ordell. My Great Grandfather Charles Bull had founded the school. He was also it's first teacher!

Many of the grade schools in western Kansas were similar and housed all eight grades in one room. The neighbors usually lived far apart. For part of one year we only had four students; we three boys and Valera Hardman! My Mom filled in for substitute teacher that year when Emma Hansen couldn't make it. I thought Mom was the best teacher ever! When Mrs. Hansen came, she would many times get there late because she had to do so many chores on their farm in the morning. That meant on cold mornings that the schoolhouse would be cold without a fire when we arrived. Willis would make a fire and yell at Merv and I to bring in wood and help. All I could seem to do was stand there and shiver. "If you would move and help, you wouldn't be so cold!" He would shout. But though I allowed he was probably right as I thought my older brother always was, I couldn't get myself to move very much. But after he got a roaring fire to going I thought it was worth all the effort, even though I only managed to bring a few sticks!

The Jones's moved onto the farm down the road and started coming to our school. I was in their house once and it was really dirty. There was only a path between the boxes and old furniture in their house. The house had a bad smell about it. Marcia and Leonard were the only two I remember, though they had other siblings. Their mother never washed their clothes and the boy's overalls would get so stiff they probably would stand alone. Leonard was always hungry and would eat erasures and drink the ink on the desks. Mrs. Hansen had no patience with him. We would have sing times and most of us memorized the songs, but Leonard couldn't do that so he would just hum along. Mrs. Hansen would stop us all suddenly to catch him humming just to make a fool of him.

During recess we would often play "ante over the schoolhouse!" The school had a high pitched roof and the idea was to barely throw the ball high enough to get over the ridge and roll down the other side to make a point. If it didn't touch the roof or it didn't make it over, that was a point lost.

Sometimes we would all come to school on our horses. Chub could outrun them all! I think Marcia had a crush on Willis but it didn't go very far with him.

KILLING RATTLESNAKES

Rattlesnakes were in abundance in western Kansas and though we had a healthy respect for them and knew their venom was dangerous and could be deadly, we did not fear them. We were part of the land and its creatures. Nothing was strange or alien to us around there. We knew of many stories of people dying from rattlesnake bites. But Dad always taught us well and taught us not to fear. He told us that fear is many times what kills. It robs you of common sense. To not get bitten by a rattler, you must know his habits and ways! And if you get bitten there are things you can do; but to run and scream would be the worst thing! Rattlers come out in the spring of the year and since they are cold blooded, they need the warmth of the sun to warm themselves, so they crawl out and stretch out in the afternoon sun. But when they hear you coming, they coil up and rattle. Though they are very dangerous, they are not treacherous. They will always rattle if they have a chance and they must be coiled up in order to strike. So you must keep your ears open and watch where you step! Many little ones come out in the spring. One week in particular coming home from school, we killed 26 rattlers of all sizes! We completely filled a fruit jar with rattles. We kept it for trophies for many years till the rattles started falling apart. To kill them we would each get a stick or rock and come up on both sides of the rattler. He would not strike until you got within striking distance, and he could not strike all three at once. While he was trying to watch all three, one of us would very quickly come in and whack him on the head with the stick or rock. Then all would join in and beat his head into the ground until we were very sure he was dead! When our dog Wolf was with us, he would help. He was very fast and would come upon the snake so fast that it didn't have time to strike, then shake it like mad until it was dead. His long fur around his neck may have saved him too!

CHAPTER SIX
Pearl Harbor!

I think not one single American my age or older will not remember very clearly the date and what he or she was doing when they heard the news of the Japanese attack on Pearl Harbor; December 7th 1941! I was seven years old and it had snowed the night before. It was very cold and that day we were waiting by the side of the road for Mrs. Hansen. She was a little late as usual but we didn't have much desire to go on foot the mile and a half through snow and then confront a cold school house, so we waited.

She stopped her car beside us in the snow and her first words as we opened the car door were, "The Japanese have bombed Pearl Harbor! It's really a terrible tragedy and many have died!" I really couldn't comprehend the entire situation at that moment, but certainly understood that it was very bad. Dad had talked about the danger of war, but it seemed to us boys a remote possibility. Many adults by then were fairly certain that the US. would get pulled in to the war. Nobody wanted it of course and there were varied feelings about it, and many families had already seen their sons called off to military service. But everyone that we knew was firmly established in the principle of defending freedom if necessary. Nobody was about to stand by forever and let a Hitler or a Tojo take over our soil or our freedom!

The people were more of one mind back then and the war united them even more. The US had stayed out of the war as long as it could even standing by while Chamberlain, the prime minister of England tried to pacify Hitler time and again believing his lies that he would not take over any more territory. Virtually the whole world stood by while Hitler took over all the Balkan Countries one by one and then France. Finally he invaded Poland and joined hands with Mussolini who was a dictator in Italy.

Japan and the Far East seemed far away, but some folks were getting nervous as Japan also showed more and more signs of land and power greed. Everyone had turned their heads for almost 40 years as Japan attacked China over and over. When they took over Manchuria and "annexed" it into the Japanese empire, everyone turned their heads the other way at the atrocities Japan committed against the Chinese people. It hardly made the news. America was tending to her own affairs. Then Japan joined hands with Hitler and Mussolini forming the "Axis". People began to say we are going to end up having to fight both sides of the world. But it still seemed unthinkable and many preferred not to think about it too much. America was not at all ready to fight a war. In World War I, Woodrow Wilson's doctrine was that this is the "War to end all wars". Since that time America had backed off from war. Why not attend to our own business? We've can produce all we need here at home! Let the rest of the world go! But sad to say, America found out that the world is not that big. And greed and hunger for power <u>cannot be satiated</u>. The more the power hungry get, the more they want!

"But Japan doesn't want us." The Far East was like another world. Though many were troubled, <u>when Japan sent a delegation to Washington to sign a peace treaty in December of that year</u>, many were happy that at least from that flank we did not have to worry!

So on December 5th the government signed a peace treaty with Japan agreeing that neither side would attack the other.

But even <u>while they were signing the treaty, Japan was fueling up their planes and loading them to the limit with bombs and bullets</u> in order to attack Pearl Harbor at dawn on Sunday morning. On December 7th they bombed the airfield and the ships and strafed everyone in sight. The Americans were not able to get their antiaircraft guns into position before it was too late. The Japanese had a total and complete victory. I don't know how many people were lost that day but <u>on the battleship Arizona alone</u>, a thousand men went down with the ship! America's entire first fleet was lost! Totally unprepared! Totally unready!.

After Pearl Harbor and as winter dragged on I remember Dad every morning listening gravely to the news of the war and what had happened the previous day. Guam, Guadalcanal. Defeat! Defeat! Defeat! I don't know how many men were lost in that first part of the war, but it was beyond comprehension. The men were not prepared and the equipment was not adequate. America's part in the war lasted only three and a half years, but America lost an average of 246 men and women per day! Over 300,000 Americans killed in the war! The price of keeping freedom in the world was tremendous!

So what was the attitude of Americans during this hard trial? That attitude shows the fiber of the American people at that time. Grit is part of it; courage another and dedication to principles. Nathan Hale, many years before when the British were ready to hang him and ask him for his last words said, "I regret that I have but one life to give for my country!"

The tremendous loss of men at Pearl Harbor and the treason by which the attack was carried out, more than any other one thing, served to galvanize the American people into action, and make them of one accord!! The war effort became a part of everyone's life. Almost every able bodied young man was taken into the armed services from ages eighteen up to twenty five. Although later on Conscientious Objectors by reason of their faith were exempted from bearing arms. The Seventh Day Adventist boys became well known for their valor, serving as medics on the line. Girls and women went to work in factories and some served in the armed forces as well, though they served in separate branches and were not on the front lines of battle zones. As the need arose the age was changed to seventeen through thirty five. My Dad wanted to go but by then he was just over age and also knew there was something else people were called to do and that was produce; both farm products and manufactured products. America won the war in part by out producing her enemies. The motto so well-known and repeated by everyone was "REMEMBER PEARL HARBOR"

Rationing was essential of goods and food such as sugar, flour, clothing, and rubber because it was needed for the war effort. No cars were manufactured for three years. The speed limit was set at 35 miles per hour on all roads. It was almost impossible to buy tires and many cars and trucks ran the entire length of the war with the same tires! Most of the people joined the effort whole heartedly because they knew it was for the common good. But some people "hoarded" the very things they were not supposed to buy in quantity. One man bought overalls every time he went to town. He ended up with a huge stack of overalls. When he died many years later, they found the stack still there. They were all rotted at creases where they were folded! The rationing was so that the production could go for the needs of the armed services.

There were some that couldn't go; because they were too young, or too old; or in some cases like our neighbor's the Walters who had five boys. The youngest was exempt because his father needed him on the farm. Dad said, "That is one boy that deserved a medal for not going." He wanted to go so badly, but knew his father needed him and knew that they had to produce wheat and meat for the war effort.

Both fronts were equally bad but I remember more vividly the war in the Pacific with Japan because some of our relatives and neighbors went there. My father's first cousin Don Paden was captured and sent to prison in Japan. Stories leaked out about torturing the war prisoners and letting them starve. (We found out after the war that it was certainly true when ex-prisoners came home) In the middle of the war a deal was made with Japan for an exchange of prisoners. Two launches capable of carrying 400 men each were to meet together at sea. A very limited amount of planes from each side was allowed to fly near there only for surveillance. But when both launches converged in the middle of the bay, the Japanese bombed both of them, so that there would be no story tellers! You can imagine how frustrated and angry everyone was about that! Our cousin Don was on that launch! With freedom only minutes away, he and all the rest of our men there were killed. The Japanese chose to kill their own men as well to hide the atrocities they were committing with the POW's! Another report came out later of a ship with something like 1800 prisoners was sunk and the guards kept the prisoners from escaping the sinking ship. Eight survived but on about two finally lived to tell about it.

The families that had boys in the service got a little flag with a blue star for each son in the service, and they would hang them in a front window. If he had died in battle the star was (gold) and if he was a prisoner of war the star was (red). Everyone respected and supported those who had sons or daughters in service.

CHAPTER SEVEN
Life on the Farm "1941"

WHEAT HARVEST

Far away from the battle field, farming was also a priority. And though the manufacturing of new farm machines had been stopped and therefore we kept using machines of an era before, the machines were kept in good order and working well.

There is nothing that typifies western Kansas more than wheat harvest. It was the most important cash crop for the farmers there and Kansas has many times been called center of the "bread basket" of the US. The manufacture of the new "combines" would have to wait so we were still using the old system. In our neighborhood we used one more time one of the big old threshing machines powered by a steam engine. The wheat was first cut with a binder. This machine cut an eight foot swath of grain and gathered it into bundles which the machine tied with twine, a heavy string. Dad always said the guy (McCormick) that invented the string tier was the smartest of the inventors. The bundles were then gathered on a big cradle on the back of the machine and when the cradle was full the operator dumped it. Each pile of bundles was the right amount to make a shock. Later the bundles were stood on end with the heads up leaning on each other forming a sort of tepee with two bundles laid on top. This was called a shock. When an entire field is shocked it makes a picturesque view but to the wheat farmers is even more beautiful because it means a prosperous year! And once the grain is in the shock, it's safer because even a hail or wind storm won't be able to destroy it, or at least not very much of it.

After the grain was allowed to dry in the shock, it would soon be time for threshing. And everyone was happy! The excitement started rising as time for threshing drew near. Wheat harvest was a really big deal with this big machine because all the neighbors had to work together to make the threshing crew large enough. I remember the last harvest with a steam engine. Both the steam engine and the thresher were very large. The threshing machine was positioned in the center of the field so that it would be the same distance from all sides of the field. A huge machine, the thresher was about 30 feet long and 8 feet high. Holes were dug for each wheel. The thresher man was very careful to get the entire machine level using a glass bubble near the top of the machine to guide him. Then the steam engine was positioned at the end of the long belt straight out from the front of the machine. The engine was also set in holes dug for the wheels so that neither the tractor nor the thresher would move. A large area was cleaned around the entire outfit down to bare earth to avoid danger of fire. The belt was crossed to make the machine turn in the right direction. The long feeder apron which had been trailed behind the machine was now hooked onto mouth of the machine and all belts were put in place on their pulleys. The huge blower pipe which had been lying on top of the machine was swung around so that it would blow the straw down wind and far away from the machine and the steam engine. A wagon or a truck was backed up to the grain spout to collect the threshed and cleaned grain. These machines did an excellent job of threshing and cleaning the wheat. A good machinist would boast that you couldn't find a grain of wheat in the straw! The wheat came out golden and beautiful. This was the fruit of a year's labor!

The bundles were loaded on large "hay" wagons pulled by a team of horses and were brought in to the machine and off loaded onto the long feeder belt which fed the threshing machine. The machine blew out the straw on one side and rolled out the golden grain from a spout high on the machine into a truck or wagon on the other side. The clean grain was hauled to the farmstead and scooped into bins or in some cases, hauled to a grain elevator. This process took nine to fourteen men, depending on the yield and availability of men. The most important man on the crew was the thresher man. He was the one who said what time to start in the morning when the grain is dry enough to thresh well and when to stop in the evening, as it begins to be too tough to thresh. He is the one that adjusts every sieve on the machine, the air fans, the threshing cylinder and checks every bearing and belt on the machine. The engine man was next as those steam engines required lots of experience and knowledge to keep them running at just the right speed all day long. I wanted so badly to be the water boy (bring drinking water to the men) but my older brothers got the job most of the time.

The noise level was high and so was the excitement level, especially for us boys. I was awed by the power of the steam engine with its two huge fly wheels cranking up the rpm on the big thresher. When a wet bundle or too many bundles at once would feed into the machine, it would groan, but the engine would just let out a puff of smoke and keep right on chugging away. A "governor" or rpm indicator on the top of the threshing machine consisting of spinning weights indicated to the thresher man if his machine was turning at the proper speed. Above all the noise and activity going on he would make eye contact with the engine man many yards away in the cab of the engine and signal to speed it up by spinning his finger or slow it down by pushing down with his hands like someone kneading bread dough. The signals were perfectly understood. The emergency stop signal was both arms raised above the head with the hands crossed. This always brought and immediate reaction as one never knew what kind of emergency might be taking place. The engine man would jerk back the throttle and throw the clutch out, the pitchers would stop pitching and all heads were on a swivel to see where the trouble was. Some part of the machine might be broken causing damage at every turn or someone might even have gotten hurt. I never saw someone get hurt but on those machines the danger was ever present.

Someone had to sleep with the outfit at night. My Dad told stories about when he was thresher man for one of his father's machines.

He would roll out his bedroll some distance from the outfit so that he would have the advantage if anyone came around at night, usually to steal tools or something. One night he woke up with someone snooping around the machine. He didn't have a gun but smoked a pipe, so he sneaked up behind the man and jammed his pipe in his back and said "Git outa here!" The guy took off running like mad!

Sometimes they threshed way up into the fall and one frosty morning he woke up with a six foot rattlesnake lying full length by his side under the covers! He had crawled in there for warmth! Needless to say, Dad slipped out of bed without disturbing his erstwhile bed partner!

In our case, they brought water for the steam engine in a tank loaded on a truck but Dad told about when he worked with his father, they had a team of beautiful Percheron horses they used to bring water from a creek for the steam engines. They pulled a water tank wagon that they would back into the water of the creek. While they hand pumped the water to fill the tank, the wheels of the cart would sink deeply into the sand. When the tank was full, he would just speak to the horses and they knew their time had come to pull that tank full of water out of there! Those mighty horses would move about in their harness to get it adjusted right and slowly start "laying in" to their load. As they increased the pressure against the load, the harness and the wood in the cart would begin to creak. Their muscles would begin to bulge and their bellies would come down closer and closer to the ground until they almost touched the ground and that heavy load would begin to move! Without another word those horses would not give up until they had pulled that heavy water wagon out of the creek!

Back to our harvest, the work started as early as possible in the morning and the days were long. A threshing machine could work longer days than a combine because the bundles were dry. These men had been up long before dawn so that they could get their chores done and be in the field before the big machine started up. Everybody took part in the harvest; if not in the field, they helped with the chores at home. Many women made the noon meal for the harvesters. The noon meal was called dinner and it was special. Those women would cook a meal in that heat that you wouldn't believe and did I ever enjoy it! Not only was the food good (the ladies outdid themselves to show what good cooks they were) but the atmosphere was almost one of celebration and great satisfaction when the harvest was good. After dinner the men would sit around and talk for a while before going back to work, and I so much enjoyed listening. Young boys were not supposed to talk too much but it was a good time to learn. I'm sure that at least some of my values of life and right and wrong were acquired during those times. The work ethic was very strong. Everyone was expected to work. But work was dignity. A farmer worked right alongside his hired hand. Work was not considered a hardship. It was a pleasure to produce!

After everyone's dinner had settled, it was time to go back to work, but not before the ladies served everyone a hot cup of coffee. Hot coffee for working in that heat? Yes, because these men worked in the heat all the time and knew what helped them the most. The hot drink puts into operation the body's self-cooling system, and there is none better. It was alright to drink cool lemonade or tea during the meal while they were sitting down in the shade, but preparing the body to go back to work in the hot sun was a different story. Hot coffee was the thing! Also the water that they drank during work was not cold, only cool because as most know who have worked hard in hot weather, cold water cuts your energy in half.

The machine worked till a little before sundown and the men had to hurry home to take care of their animals and in many cases, milk their cows. Those who had boys big enough to help but too young for the armed services had help at home.

After one farm was finished, the machine was moved to the next farm in line. I don't know how they decided the order in which each farmer's crop was threshed but it didn't seem to be a problem. Moving the machine was a lot of work and everyone took part. The machine had to be thoroughly cleaned out, the big blower pipe rolled around and laid on top of the machine and the long feeder apron unhooked from the mouth of the machine, rolled around behind and hooked on the back like a trailer. Many belts were taken off and rolled up; the steam engine turned around and hooked onto the tongue of the machine. The huge engine with the big machine hooked on to it and the feeder apron hooked on behind the machine made a very long train and took a large area to turn around. This whole process was repeated until all the farmers of that area had threshed their grain. Some times a month or two. The field looked different now, no shocks left standing and only the straw pile as a reminder of the year's harvest. The straw would be put to good use as bedding for the livestock this coming winter.

Little did I know it at that time but I was witnessing the very end of an era. An era prolonged because of the years of depression and then the war effort. That was the last year I ever saw a farm steam engine in operation. It was also the last year I saw one of those huge threshing machines work. Combines would soon be taking over the harvesting process; the first ones were pulled by a tractor before the self-propelled ones were invented. The stationary threshing process continued where necessary, but with much smaller machines and gasoline tractors to power them.

GOING TO NORTON

Dad kept increasing his dairy herd and each morning and evening after milking we would separate the cream from the fresh milk with a hand-cranked milk separator. The separator had a little bell on the crank handle and we turned the crank faster and faster till the bell quit dinging. Then we could open the little spigot of the milk tank to let it flow through the spinning disks. As the milk spins in the machine the cream comes to the top since it is lighter than milk. So the milk came out the bottom spout and we fed that to the calves and hogs. The cream came out the top spout and that we saved to take to town on Saturday. The milk that wasn't fed to the calves and hogs was left to "clabber" (form cakes) and later fed to the chickens. Clabbered milk made really good pancakes too! Mom's chicken project was also important. The folks bought a "brooder" and with that we hatched leghorn chickens, about half would be roosters and half pullets. They ran loose during the day and would range all over the farm yard, utilizing the barnyard manure pile as part of their food plus the barley we would throw out to them in the afternoon and the clabbered milk. At night we would shut them up so the coyotes wouldn't get them. The pullets would start laying after about six months and we would start catching up the roosters for fryers when they would dress out at two pounds.

On Saturday we would take the cream and eggs to town. We would take a case of eggs which was thirty six dozen and many times a half case as well which was eighteen dozen, fifty four dozen eggs plus the cream production of the week. Things were looking a lot better now. That of course is not high production compared to today's standards but the most of the chicken feed and cattle feed didn't cost anything.

Dad bought a little blue International pickup. It didn't start very good in the winter, but it sure was pretty! It was twelve miles to Norton and eleven miles to Lenora, but we did most of our "trading" in Norton. It was six miles of dirt road and six miles of "oiled" road. The cab was narrow so we boys rode in the back. The folks would sometimes let us boys go to the "picture show" while they were shopping. The shows scared me and I never liked them because I was afraid they would wreck the cars in the city traffic and I never liked the love scenes, but I would have to go with my brothers.

Buying clothes and shoes for us boys always had to be "equal". Each boy had to receive the same in shirts, pants or shoes. Because we went barefoot all summer and our feet would spread out wide they would not fit well into new shoes. My feet were exceptionally wide and the salesman would feel of my toes and say, "these shoes are fine, there is room for his toes to grow. But my feet were so wide that the problem was the width. So we would leave the store with the new shoes on and soon I would start to cry because the shoes were hurting my feet so bad. So we would have to go back and look for bigger shoes that were wide enough for my feet!

I loved the trip back after dark. Mom would bring blankets and make a bed in the back of the pickup and we could lie there looking up at the constellations in the heavens. It was beautiful! When we got home after dark, we had to milk the cows, shut up the chickens and "slop" the hogs. I learned to milk when I was six years old on an old gentle cow that was almost dry, but I probably just helped with the other chores on those nights. All together we did the chores in a short time and Mom would have hot milk and bread for supper. I loved that!

MONTGOMERY WARD

We called it "Monkey Wards" and they had a mail order department. Each year they sent out a big catalog with all kinds of "goodies" listed. From the time we sent in the order till the merchandise arrived took about two weeks. What a long two weeks it was! I remember when "tennis" shoes first came out and we ordered some for each of us boys for school! It seemed like they would never come! At that time that mail order company filled a need in rural America making all kinds of different merchandise available to the farmers. Besides, last year's catalog served as toilet paper! We never bought rolls of toilet paper back then.

PATTY

When I was eight our sister Patty was born. Doc Stephenson was her doctor too but now our house was a lot better and the weather was nicer than it had been eight years before when I was born, even though it was also in August. We boys were sent up to visit the Keever's for the night, so that was a treat for us. We boys had dug a square hole in the yard for kind of a den and Dad for some reason never complained about that hole in the yard. The next morning after Patty was born the hole was strangely filled up! After Patty was born Mom had to stay in bed for ten days by doctor's orders because in those days they believed it was necessary. By the end of ten days of course the mother was so weak from inactivity that she would get dizzy just by sitting up so they were sure that she should have stayed in bed even longer! The folks hired a girl to help Mom, and she was a character. A city girl, she had a hard time adjusting to farm life. She would sing, "I'm going out to the farm to milk the cows and chickens!" I don't know if she was much help for Mom.

FIRE IN THE PORCH!

It was a cold Monday morning in the winter. Monday was wash day no matter how cold it was. Sometimes the wash would freeze on the line, but it would freeze dry in about two days, so then Mom would bring it in, and thaw it out by the stove and it would be already fairly dry. But wash we must on Monday morning! The wash room was a closed in part of the porch. This particular morning as usual we three boys were carrying water from the stock tank to fill the washer and all the rinse tubs which were setting on benches. The gasoline engine that powered the washer was hard to start when it was cold, so they had put a kerosene lantern next to it to warm it up. Willis was filling the little engine with gas when he accidentally tipped over the lantern. The gasoline exploded into fire! Frightened, he dumped the whole tub of water on the fire thinking it would surely put out the fire. Just the opposite happened; the water spread the kerosene and gasoline and the fire all over the room!

Dad came running and decided since the fire was already spread over the whole room by water; our only chance was to put it out with more water. He commanded us all to carry water as fast as we could from the stock tank, about twenty yards away. And carry we did! I had never been so frightened before! Little baby Patty was inside the house and I kept thinking about her and when we should quit fighting the fire to save her! But praise God! After what seemed like an eternity but really was only about ten or fifteen minutes, Dad had doused the fire completely and we and our house and family were all safe! I learned from my Dad that in an emergency, there is almost always something you can do to better or save the situation and that you must do with all your might!

TELEPHONE!

Neither telephones nor electricity had come to that rural area yet. Electricity would not arrive for many years, but it was possible to bring a telephone line in. So several neighbors got together, bought the wire necessary, put up the poles along the fence lines and brought the phone line out all the way from Lenora, 11 miles away. Our "party line" had seven families. The telephone was a large box about eight inches wide, four inches deep and sixteen inches high. On the left side hung the receiver which when it was lifted up, put you on the line; the local party line that is. The speaker stuck out of the front of the box at the end of a black pipe. There was a little crank handle on the right side of the box that when you turned it rang "Central" or one of your party line members. Each one on the party line had a different ring, two longs, two shorts, etc. but many times others would listen in when they heard another being called. I remember Mom saying, "Emma are you rubbering?" that was the word for listening in when they weren't supposed too! Emma Hansen was our school teacher, a good woman but very curious! To get anyone outside your party line you had to call Central, (one long) and ask her to make the call for you. If the central (operator) needed to call everybody for an emergency, she would give seven longs, then it was legal for everyone to lift up the receiver because it was an emergency or an extremely important announcement.

HORSES AND THINGS

After school started we weren't riding Chub. She got sick and we didn't know it. She had cancer of the uterus and it had gotten bad. Dad called the vet and had him put her down to save the agony. The first we knew about it was that she was gone. Dad had buried her before he told us to make it easier for us.

About then the old mare had a colt and for me that kind of took the place of Chub. The colt became a real pet. When winter came, Dad turned the mare and colt out to pasture and I forgot about the colt. One day in the Spring I was coming home from school and the mare with her colt were there in the corner of the pasture close to the road. I crossed the fence to pet the colt. She let me pet her easy enough but then turned to run away and kicked up her heels. One landed squarely in my mouth, taking out two teeth on the bottom, and splitting my upper lip. Dad took me to Doc Stephenson in Lenora and he sewed up my lip.

Then later in the summer I was playing with an old wheelbarrow wheel on which the rim was broken in two with one side higher than the other. I was running along supporting my hands on the axle. The wheel hit a rock and bounced up and caught my top front tooth and jerked it out. I cried like a baby not for the pain but because I had lost another tooth. (Had we known in that moment, the tooth could have been put back in and survived.) So now I had three teeth missing in front.

CHAPTER EIGHT
We Move to Colorado

In the early spring of 1944, we moved to Colorado because Mom had asthma real bad and many times suffered attacks and could hardly breathe. It seemed they were getting worse. I guess nobody knows what an asthmatic suffers except other asthmatics. The doctors couldn't seem to help much and they were told that on the high plains of Colorado the air was much dryer and it would be better there. Our grandparents on Mom's side had already moved to Colorado and we could maybe find a place close to them.

Dad and Uncle Harold took a trip to Colorado and were able to rent a farm. So plans were made for moving! Merv was really anxious to move, but I loved it in here and didn't want to leave these Kansas hills and prairies. I don't think Willis wanted to leave either. But move we did. We took all the furniture and household goods in one trip and then Dad was to come back to get the livestock. We had a car and a truck then. Dad drove the truck and Willis helped Mom drive the car. I think he was thirteen that year. Mom "jawed" at him most of the time he drove!

EAST OF GREELEY

In Colorado we didn't have a telephone but we had electricity! Each room just had one bare bulb in the center of the ceiling, but all you had to do was pull the light cord and the light came on! That was really marvelous for us!

School in Colorado at first was hard for me. I was in the middle of the fourth grade and they were doing four digit multiplication. Math had never been hard for me, but I had missed out when they first explained multiplying multiple numbers. The teacher was giving whole pages of problems for homework. If you didn't get yesterday's homework finished, it was added to today's homework. I couldn't get done and my homework kept piling up till I had several pages to do. The burden kept getting bigger and bigger and it was like I was sinking into a black pit and going down further all the time. Finally the teacher realized my predicament and forgave me my past homework! It was like I had a new lease on life! She took some time to explain how to do the problems and from then on, I had no trouble. That was one of my first lessons on the power of forgiveness.

At that time there were still many Model A Fords in service. Granddad had one that was like new. And there were still a few Model T Fords around and they moved much more slowly than other cars. It was spring and it had snowed just enough to make snowballs. We had two miles to walk on the road and it was fun to throw snowballs after the cars that went by. One of the neighbors went by in a "Model T" Ford, a two seater with a high flat back. Merv threw a good one after him, but didn't calculate how slow the car was going. The snowball hit the flat back of the Model T with a resounding boom! There was nothing slow however about the reactions of the driver. He stopped that machine so fast and was out of there and yelling at Merv before he had a chance to hide or run! We all got a lesson on respect and care of other people's property! I never forgot it!

This school was much larger than the ones we were used to in Kansas. It had several class rooms and an auditorium. We were having an all-school assembly and I was sitting on the center aisle. For some reason I thought I was really cute that day and was acting silly and giggling about myself. What I didn't know was that the principal was coming up behind me! He grabbed me up in one movement and carried me out to the hall. There he gave me a very good spanking that straightened me up like magic! I learned to be quiet in the assemblies!

It was a hard year on this farm we rented. It wasn't the best. The soil was very alkaline and the best field was infested with bindweed, which choked out the corn plants. The cows were giving milk but the barn wasn't good enough to sell Grade A milk so we had to sell Grade

B which was much cheaper. Even though we had irrigation water, the crops didn't do all that well. Willis worked out putting up hay. I liked that when he would tell about it even though I never went with him. The man was a prosperous farmer as many were in that area. They had huge white barns for hay and cattle and big white two story houses. It impressed me that this farmer's wife worked in the field with him and before going to work put the dinner in the oven of one of these new electric stoves and set the timer so that dinner would be ready and hot at twelve noon! For us who didn't even have electricity before, it was like they were living in another world!

Dad did some custom combining with his machine that year. He would take me with him to move the truck up to the machine when the bin was full. All I had to do was wait till Dad signaled me to come, start the truck, put it in power low (first gear), let out the clutch and go slowly toward the machine. When I got close Dad took over. Real simple but I considered it driving. I thought, I've got to remember this, I started driving when I was ten years old! I had just turned ten.

DANGER IN THE DRAIN DITCH

One afternoon, we three boys went swimming in a nice water hole right at a road intersection. A drain ditch came up at an angle and crossed under the intersection on diagonally through a metal culvert about 24" in diameter; and 50 feet long. It had a good downgrade slope and the water was up over the top edge of the culvert so a very large amount of water was passing through there and the suction was at its maximum. Little did we think about that though, and once when Willis passed by too closely, he was sucked up against the round opening. He was strong enough that the water did not immediately pull him in but neither could he move away. Merv came right to his rescue and I jumped out of the water, thinking to run for help. Then I realized our house was almost a mile away and would never get help in time, so I ran back to help, then I thought, no I must run for help, and by that time my mind was in complete panic. I ended up running back and forth screaming. Of course that just made matters worse but Willis and Merv kept struggling together until they managed to get him free! What a tremendous relief! Needless to say we didn't go back in to swim there again.

We went home and climbed up into the big tree in the front yard and talked in low tones. Mom said later that she suspected that something had happened but we never talked about till years later. But I resolved in my heart NEVER to let my mind go into panic again! Dad had taught In every critical situation there is something you can do to help. And you must do the best you can! Merv did that and I didn't! Now Merv had saved both Willis and I from drowning!

OFF LIMITS

The Union Pacific Railroad ran across one corner of the farm and one day a nice new car with some important looking men came to visit us. They were officials from the Railroad! Merv had showed me a very interesting little trick. When the passenger train came through at five o'clock in the afternoon, we would put little rocks on the rails and watch them explode when the train went over them! Every day we would put a few more rocks, until the day they came to visit us. That put an end to our little railroad adventure! The Railroad people seemed to take the care of their rails seriously!

CHAPTER NINE
West of Denver

WASHOUT

From Greeley we moved to west Denver. The school we went to was named Washington Heights but everyone called it "Washout". Between classes the school grounds were run by tough kids. I don't remember that there was ever once an adult out there. The boys ran the school grounds and there was a hierarchy established by fist fighting and threats. There were definite rules established and governed by the kids. You couldn't hit below the belt; you couldn't use any kind of weapon, you couldn't hit someone who had glasses on, a rock inside the fist was considered bad. The toughest guy in school was Allen Cagle and he was the undisputed "president". He took a liking to me and took me under his wing and taught me how to fight. I was in the fifth grade and small for my age but strong for my size. Mostly because I was Allen Cagle's friend I was considered tough too. Every recess and noon hour were occupied by fights or threats of fights. That was the extent of the "Washout" "sports" program!

But on our first day of school there, I didn't feel very tough. It was an old building and the wood floors sloped from back to front of our room. I was placed on the back row and needed to go to the bath room in the worst way but didn't know the rules whether you could just get up and go or ask permission in front of everyone. Either way, I was afraid to take the risk so decided to try to hold it till the end of class. Well, that didn't happen and after agonizing for half an hour, I finally let go. I discovered much to my dismay that the floor not only sloped toward the front but also toward the middle of the room. My pee ran all the way down the room to in front of the teacher's desk. I was so mortified that after that my mind was kind of in a blur. The kids began to snicker and I hoped that they wouldn't realize where it came from.

But the teacher did and she excused me to go home. The next day she kindly explained to me that all I had to do was raise my hand with one finger up for number one and two fingers up for number two and I would be excused to go and do that!

They did have school lunch, and it was good food. The leftovers were put in a five gallon "slop" bucket along with water from washing dishes and the bigger boys had to take turns when school let out to carry out the "slop" bucket and dump it out by the edge of the school grounds.

We did enjoy learning a new sport when we lived on West Third. There was a pretty little lake on our way to school and after it started to freeze over, we would go there on week-ends and during winter vacation to ice skate. That's where I learned to ice skate with the neighbor kids (not the fighty ones) and we would have a great time skating there.

We lived in a cinder block house and it was damp in the winter. One night I had what might have turned into asthma if it hadn't been for my Dad's help, comfort and wisdom. He sat down beside the bed and "coached" me on how to breathe. He said, "just be calm and breathe slowly. Don't get excited, just breathe slow and easy." With that I started breathing easier and went to sleep. I learned that my nerves were closing up my wind pipe, and that was a big part of the problem.

THE SELANDER PLACE

That Spring Dad rented a 320 acre farm on South Federal at the west edge of Denver. East of the road was all residential and on the west side was this beautiful farm with a big white house and two huge white barns with silos. We lived in the tenant house in the back of the farm yard, but it was an adequate house for our family, with electricity and an inside bathroom. It was a good farm with deep black soil and I really liked it there. Selander's daughter had horses and she would let us ride them sometimes. Dad hired a man, Orley Nutt. He had been in the army and was good with machinery. I kind of idolized him and thought he must know about everything. But his personal life was a mess. When he said he'd been married five times, we couldn't believe it!

The farm was all planted to hay and corn and barley. We all took part in the hard work. My part was still the smallest since I was the youngest. Dad kept Willis out of school that year to plow. He was plowing with one of Selander's crawler tractors. Some of the neighbors exclaimed that they thought the tractor didn't have a driver since he was pretty small yet and his head barely showed above the seat!

SEEK THE LORD

We started to go to church that year and I'm sure God was working; especially in my parents. The Baptist pastor, Joe Gooden was on fire for God and as he got warmed up with the sermon he would first take off his coat, then loosen his tie, then he would take it off! I remember that more than I remember what he preached about. All three of us boys were baptized that year, though judging from our lives later, I don't think we were "born again". But I know that God and the Bible were made more real to me then. Besides God was truly moving in the family and it was a good year. Our family was more united and we had an excellent crop. The Lord protected it even though there were three bad hail storms that year. The farm was a mile long north to south and one half mile wide east to west. The first hail storm in June came along the north side and got just about 20 yards into the field of hay, damaging only a small part of one cutting. The second hail storm, a bad one, came in July, when the grain was getting ripe. The edge of the storm went down the entire west side from south to north and just barely got over into the irrigation ditch on our side and it did us no damage! Then in the fall there was another storm that just touched the south side, getting into the corn field at the end of the rows. It did very little damage. The Lord had saved our crops and that year the folks made enough money to make a good down payment on a farm of our own, which also was 320 acres near the town of Fort Lupton. The Lord had been good to us that year!

CHAPTER TEN
Fort Lupton

THE DAIRY FARM

After moving to Fort Lupton we got too busy and had no time for the Lord, and the year my little brother Richard was born, we again had three hail storms, but they hit us square! One in the spring that took the barley crop and damaged the first cutting of hay. Then another one in July that took the second cutting of hay and the wheat. Then the worst one was right after Rich was born, August 18th. It took the corn crop.. I remember because Mom and baby Richard were still in the hospital.. We had to put pillows against the north windows to keep them from breaking in with the hail beating against them! I never realized the Lord's dealings until years later when Dad said, "Whenever I remembered the Lord, He was good to me but when I forgot the Lord, he forgot me!" And I began to think how that God had spared us three hail storms on West Federal and then three hail storms had hit us square at Fort Lupton. As one of Martin Luther's songs go, "He hastens and chastens, His will to make known."

Dad had planned for years and bred his cattle to get a Grade A dairy herd. I loved planning and building. Even when I was in the second and third grades my day-dreams were all about setting up a big cattle operation. I would plan how to make all the granaries and hay barns in a square protecting the yard in the middle from the fierce winter winds and cold. I would plan a system for moving all the feed by augers and belts to mix it and then send it on to the cattle feeders. So when Dad would talk about his plans for the corrals, loafing shed and Grade A milk barn, I was very enthusiastic about it!

So even though Dad did most of the work while we were in school and in fact we all had the measles that year and each took his turn to spend two weeks in bed, we felt part of all this work. He remodeled the barn, built the corrals and a cattle loafing shed. This place was ideal for a stock farm. It had creek bottom land that was self-irrigated and made excellent pasture. And though the sandy ground would not yield the highest production, it was just about right for producing all the hay and winter feed we needed for the dairy.

THE BUNK HOUSE

The house only had two bedrooms so we boys used the bunk house that was about five long steps from our back porch. It was an old building painted yellow just like the house, but not at all insulated. It had two rooms. We used the back room for storage and the front room for our bedroom. The furniture was simple; a double bed, a pot-bellied stove and a couple of old chairs. The three of us slept in one bed. There was none other. We all had to turn the same way. If one of us wanted to turn the other way, he had to get the agreement of the other two! But you might guess who decided! It was Willis! As usual, Merv was always in the middle. When it got cold in the winter we would start a fire in the pot-bellied stove. It would get red hot and fairly jump from the draft of the fire. When it got hot in there, we would all jump in bed and cover up, and soon begin to hear the cold creep into the building as the stove burned up the cottonwood and began to cool down. As the wood in the walls began to shrink from the cold, the boards would let out pops and snaps and we could literally feel the cold creep into the room. The secret was for us to warm up the bed before it got too cold.

When it snowed during the night and the wind blew, the snow would come in through the cracks and make lines across the floor and up onto the bed. So when Dad called us in the morning from the house, we would jump out of bed, grab our clothes and dash out the bunk house in our skivvies and make the five strides to the back porch of the house in about two seconds and through the kitchen door to a warm house. We would stand by the nice fire in the living room stove and dress. But breakfast was not yet. We had to milk the cows and feed the calves first. And there was no time to lose either because the School

Bus would be coming by to pick us up at ten minutes after eight. We were milking about twenty cows at first; The cows were divided up between Dad and we three boys according to the ability and age of each. I milked two cows at first, then three and when I got up to four cows, Dad got an electric milking machine. Our herd grew to 35 cows in all with about twenty four in production at any one time. We had three machines and each one milked two cows at a time. So it went pretty fast. The corrals and hay stack area were well arranged so that feeding the cows and calves didn't take long. We fed the little calves skim milk and milk replacer. We would teach them to drink out of a bucket by getting them to suck our fingers and then put our fingers under the milk. After several tries, they would get the idea and drink straight out of the bucket. When they were five months old they would be weaned to eat grain and hay.

How nice it was to come in after chores were done to the smell of breakfast getting ready. Breakfast was always a big deal on the farm and we were hungry by then, but first we had to quickly wash up and change to school clothes. At breakfast we boys would usually get into a big discussion, (you might call them arguments!) Our neighbor from across the road, Bill Owens was an auctioneer. Many times he would drop in to have a cup of coffee while we were eating breakfast. He auctioneered at a little used item auction in Fredrick, six miles west of us in the evenings. He was quite a story teller and I liked to listen to him, but Dad would get impatient because when it was time to go to work he would still be talking! I remember how he would laugh at our arguments and say, "You boys have any words fore yu fell out?" About that time Mr. Riley's school bus would be coming and we would hear him start beeping the horn way down the road. So we would jump up and grab our things as fast as possible and run out putting on our coats. I don't think we ever managed or even thought about trying to be out there waiting for him to come. The bus ride was about forty minutes and we got a chance to see how the neighbors and the families of our school mates were doing. Mr. Riley had heat in the bus but it wasn't the best so we had to be dressed warmly.

We had a big pile of ear corn out near the barn that year. One night it snowed about three inches early in the night. It stopped about midnight. The next morning Dad found tracks coming into the yard and a little hole in the corn pile where Bill Owens had helped himself to some corn for his calves. Dad commented, Now I know why Bill always talks about picking up "this or that" at the sale. It's because he probably doesn't pay for it! He never said anything to Bill about the corn. He said, His kind won't steal enough to hurt you if your his "friend". I learned a little about human nature from that!

SUMMER TIME

Everybody took part in the work except Patty and Rich because they were too small. Mom was very busy with two little ones as well a cooking for a "hungry crew". There was plowing and planting in the spring, then putting up hay. The second cutting of hay and grain harvest came right in there together so it was the busiest time. The hay was cut and raked into windrows and when it was dry, we stacked it in huge stacks in the stack yard near the corrals. We used a buck rake pushed by an old truck turned around backwards, with the buck rake attached to what had been the rear end and now was the front end. We put up hay together with Uncle Harold and our cousins. Willis and Lloyd Thiesen ran the buck rakes since they were the oldest. They brought it in to the stack where the "stacker" was set up. The stacker was like a huge fork made of wood on a framework anchored firmly and hinged to raise up and throw its load onto the stack. This was done by a system of pulleys and a cable pulled by a pickup or a good horse. The buck rakes would unload onto the stacker, then someone would back up the pickup to raise the huge stacker fork until it was straight up and had deposited its load onto the stack. Forming the stack and walking down the hay was hard work.

In spite of all the work we had, we still had energy left for exploring the countryside at night with our dog, Wolf. At night the countryside seemed more exciting, romantic, almost enchanted. One night we were coming back home from exploring a little lake not far from our farm, when all of a sudden we heard a great battle begin. We couldn't see what was going on at first but the battle seemed to be moving toward a creek that ran close by. When we got there we found that Wolf had tangled with a big raccoon. Although outweighed by the dog, the coon was in command. He had deliberately taken the dog over to the creek and with himself on the bottom, was pulling the dog down under the water! The coon could easily last twice as long as the dog under water and thereby drown him! We had to kill the coon to rescue the dog. We thought we knew all about country and its animals but we learned that night about coons! We thought it would be great to have a coonskin but had no idea how hard it would be to skin it. I ended up working on it several nights till the coon got so ripe I couldn't stand it any longer.

My brothers, cousins and their friends the Rogers all ran around together and I would tag along. Some summer nights we would go swimming, play basketball in our yard or the older boys would put on boxing gloves and have a match. Mitch Rogers was the biggest among us and once he challenged Dad. Neither one was a boxer so they just had a pummeling match! It didn't last very long but they really went round and round for a little bit! Neither one of them ever challenged the other again! I guess once was enough!

BICYCLE ACCIDENT

Our farm was three and a half miles from town and I had had been riding a bike to school because I had a job after school cleaning out the ashes and basement of the John Deere Implement store. They had a big coal furnace in the basement. It was hard work but I really appreciated the money they paid me, (fifty five cents). It was my first job and it gave me some spending money. Afterwards I would ride my bike north through town to the Sugar Factory, turn left and cross the river, go the three miles west to Sickler's farm, then north for a half mile to our place.

It was beet harvest time and the heavily loaded beet trucks were bringing their loads to the beet dump behind the factory. The farmers south of town were obliged to go through town. Most of them went quite slowly and though we knew we weren't supposed to, we would many times hang on to the back right hand corner of a truck and let it tow us along! If they didn't have a right hand mirror, which many didn't, the truck driver would never realize we were there. So as I turned north on Main Street and a particularly slow truck came by. I hooked on to it and coasted all the way to where he and I would both turn west. As he passed the factory he slowed down even more, almost to a stop. I crossed behind him thinking he would take time in making the corner and I would just get ahead of him. At that very moment a car was coming fast from the north and hit me just as I came out from behind the truck. A man working in the factory at that moment told me later that I bounced off the hood of the car and flew up fifteen feet into the air like a football that had been kicked.

I don't remember being hit and I woke up much later lying on my back. It was dark. I could hear my Dad talking to me. He said we had to wait for the "ambulance" to come. The town coroner also provided the ambulance service. That was customary back then. He would be on the scene to declare dead those who died and take the living to the hospital! He also had a funeral home! He was out of town when they called him. The garage owner nearby, who called my Dad and the coroner, was wise enough not to move me from the ground till someone arrived who had knowledge of first aid procedures. When the coroner arrived, he knew just what to do. The nearest hospital was in Brighton, eight miles south. My right arm was broken and doubled back with the bone protruding out of the skin, called a compound fracture. The "hospital" was really a house converted to hospital use. I thought the nurse was the prettiest thing. (Years later I wondered why) But she was really nice and explained how I needed to breathe the gas deeply so I would go to sleep and they could set the bone and repair the arm. The doctor, whom I don't remember at all, did an excellent job and I never had trouble with that arm and the scar all but disappeared!

CHIP

Bud Owen, our neighbor's son was a trucker and a horse trader. Dad bought a young gelding from him. He said, "He's green broke, so he'll be alright for the boys." Both Willis and Merv were more interested in other things so I kind of "inherited' him by default. He was much more green than broke! Besides he was of Appaloosa blood, a nervous, high strung breed that never becomes very docile. But I loved that horse and we made friends. When I set foot in the stirrup or jumped on him bareback however, I had to be ready to ride because he was on his way! Not knowing much about training horses, I never taught him to be led by a halter or to stand still while I mounted him. I never tried to make him too gentle. That way, he was more of a "one man horse" and I was proud of that. Of course it was a mistake not to teach him to lead by the halter, but since I was the only one riding him, when I would catch him up, I would jump on his back instead of leading him in to the corral. We had and understanding! He was tall and liked to run and I liked that too. He would go like the wind. We had great times together, he and I exploring the countryside.

On one of my cross country rides I started to cross an old fence with him and he hooked a hind foot in a loop of loose barbed wire. I got off and tried to lead him across but he just trembled. I couldn't get him to lift his foot up and out of the wire. There is a very great danger with horses caught in wire as they soon panic and begin to kick and fight the wire, usually ending up cutting a foot off or mangling themselves to the point that they have to be "put away" before they can be stopped. The only thing that was keeping him from panicking at this moment was my voice because he trusted me. But I knew that I only had a short time that I could keep him calm and as soon as he started kicking, there would be no stopping him. I decided since he had learned to be confident in me when I was on his back and had never learned to be led, I must get on his back, take up the reins and talk him out of this. It was a calculated risk because I wasn't at all sure he would obey me well enough to pick his foot out of the loop in the wire and pick the remaining back foot up high enough to clear the wire! So talking to him in soothing tones all the while, I carefully got on his back. That wasn't so simple either as he was tall and to get on (he wasn't saddled) I had to first jump up and get my elbows hooked over his back and then swing my right foot across his rump. This was always the signal for him to take off! So I stroked his neck and talked to him while I got into position. I jumped up and he didn't move, just trembled! But he seemed to understand that he didn't dare move till I told him to and trusted in me to get him out of this! So after I got on, I continued talking to him and stroking his neck. I said, "Now lift your foot, Chip, easy boy." I was praying as best I could at that point in my life. Chip obeyed me! He lifted his foot very carefully and it cleared the wire. "Now the other foot, easy boy!" and he gingerly raised his other foot and came clear of the wire! Needless to say, I didn't come back through that way!

About two years later another incident didn't turn out so well though. It was the last day of the school year and a traditional day for the students to go on an outing after receiving their report cards. That particular year a number of us planned to go horseback riding. I put the saddle on Chip and went to Counter's house where we were to meet. It turned out that no one else showed up. Their daughter Ann and I were good friends but never went out together much. My friend Johnny Norris and I would spend a lot of time at their house. If she wasn't home we would talk to her mother and eat cinnamon toast! Her mother had confidence in me and let Ann go with me riding behind the saddle on Chip.

Not long after we left the Counter farm, we crossed the Platte River on a very narrow and long bridge. The river was high and the water was swirling very close to the bottom of the bridge. When we were half way across, at the very worst place for Chip because of the water, a pickup entered at the far end. A farmer who knew nothing about horses, not only did not stop, he didn't even slow down! It was a one lane bridge with planks in the middle for vehicles to cross on. By the side of these planks there was barely room for a horse. But though I tried to hold him over to the side, he would swing his rump out into the way of the oncoming pickup. I would straighten him up again but the moment the pickup got close, Chip felt frightened and again swung his rump into the path of the pickup. Fortunately Ann's leg was not crushed but Chip was hit square in the flank and his leg buckled under the wheel. After the pickup passed, we both slid off and poor Chip was standing there with his left rear leg hanging out crooked like some appendage that didn't belong to him! I was so frustrated and sad that I couldn't say anything. Someone called our folks. Dad came with a veterinarian who said there was nothing he could do for Chip because a horse will not stand still for his leg to heal. So they decided to put him to sleep. Dad said, "You go on home, I know you won't want to watch this." I didn't want to watch it. Someone took us home. I can't remember who, I was so sad.

THE DAIRY IS GONE!

The Colorado air didn't have the healing effect that they had hoped it would for Mom. It seemed that her asthma kept getting worse. They decided that she would take a battery of tests in a clinic in Denver. So she spent several days there and their conclusion was that the very worst thing for her asthma was cow hair; and that was what we had the most of around there! I know Dad was so very discouraged and one day he loaded up the whole herd of dairy cows and took them to the sale barn. The cows were "Milking Shorthorns", a breed that Dad had worked many years in gathering together and breeding. He was breeding a cow whose calf was much better for beef than the Holstein and whose milk was rich in butterfat, something that at that point in time brought a better price for the milk. But at the sale barn they sold for low grade beef, about as cheap as you can get. Years of work and planning dumped all at once. It was so disappointing for all of us when we came home from school and there were no cows!

The folks sold the south eighty acres with the house. The best land on the farm, and bought a house on the edge of Fort Lupton. The place had an acre of land, but the lower half had been a junk yard so though it was covered over with dirt, it would only serve as a corral for the one cow we kept, old Strawberry. The place had a small barn. We used one side for a garage. The other side had a hay mow, room for some feed storage and a stall for old Strawberry. I ended up being in charge of milking and had to be very careful to change clothes and wash my hands to avoid that contact with Mom. We sold two quarts a day to the Meikles family. After I milked in the evening I would strain the milk and put two quarts of it out on the front porch and when Mr. Meikle came home from working in the coal mine, he would pass by our house and stop and pick up the two jars of milk. That worked pretty well and Mrs. Meikle would stop by and pay us once a month for the milk.

I was in the ninth grade when we moved to town and this was the beginning of a new phase in my life. We still had the farm, 240 acres of it and that would still be our principle occupation for now. Dad said, "Well, I guess I'll just have to learn to be a suitcase farmer" belittling his situation. He bought another tractor; an "A" John Deere. I admire at how much work we did with such little horsepower back then. The "A" had 28 horsepower and our "B" only had 18 horsepower and neither tractor had lights! Now days anything less than 40 horsepower just won't do! Dad rented more land and we farmed over 700 acres that year. That fall Willis joined the Air Force and Merv started working away from home, so it was the last year we all farmed together. Soon Merv joined the Air Force as well, so only Dad and I farmed together.

I have good memories of those years that we farmed while living at the edge of town. I bought another horse, a young mare that I broke and trained. I called her Babe. She was a nice little horse, but nothing compared to Chip.

CHAPTER ELEVEN
Learning Business and People

The Greeley Tribune offered me a chance to make some money delivering their newspaper. I had to look for my own customers as that Paper hadn't had much distribution in Fort Lupton before that. It was good practice for me to learn to deal with people, to convince them to buy the paper and then deliver it faithfully each week day. I learned about people who pay well and those that don't. Some I had to catch on their payday while they still had money. I also learned to deal with dogs. Some were downright mean. But I learned that even those would not stand up to someone who was not afraid of them. You had to look them straight in the eye and command them without fear. I did carry an iron pipe in my paper bag just in case. I never had to use it but would hold it in my hand when facing the really bad dogs.

About that time there arose a great contention between the white kids and the Mexican children of immigrants who came to seek work in the US. There were prejudges on both sides, we called them "Spicks" which originated from their way of saying "speak". There arose a subculture that was looking for trouble. It may have originated as a manner of self-identity, but it became dangerous. But at the same time there were a number of kids of Mexican descent in my class at school, probably eight or ten, all well accepted and their parents had homes or farms in the area. We also had a number of Japanese in our class, also well accepted, a very hard working and industrious people. Most were farmers. Young people can be careless or even callous in the way they treat others, but don't usually have a natural racial prejudice. That comes from circumstances or from the parents. The majority of the kids who were causing problems either didn't attend school or came from Denver.

On Sunday afternoons many of the young people would gather around the Cozy Corner Drug store and soda fountain to talk, play the pin ball games and drink soda. Some of those people began to frequent that area also. Since I would pass through their neighborhood each day delivering papers and carried that iron pipe in my bag, they picked me out as someone to pick a fight with. One Sunday they gathered a group of toughs to challenge me. I decided not to fight there and then as the odds were too great. I was standing in front of the plate glass window of the drug store and one kept trying to hit me. My reflexes were so fast that I could dodge his fist each time and he would hit the window. Since I didn't fight back the others couldn't find a reason to join in the flay.

I waited my time, and found it one day in the movie house lobby when I found the same boy alone. I took him into the bath room and worked him over. Shortly after that I was sitting in the Movie and one of their group wised off behind me and I turned around and smacked him on the nose. After that they didn't bother me anymore. I continued to ride my bike with papers through their neighborhood and they never again bothered me.

But a greater storm was brewing as more of the gang from Denver heard about it and challenged the "white" kids of Fort Lupton to a gang fight. Mom wouldn't let me go to town that night and it was probably better. The Mexicans were on one side of the street and the "white" kids on the other. Harlan Miller probably saved the night as much as the good police effort. He had a spray can with ammonia and when a fight was brewing would sneak up and with one spray would take the fight out of everybody! We never heard any more about the Denver gang. Evidently the law enforcement was more effective back then.

My other project was rabbits. With those two projects I bought my own clothes and paid my own expenses through school. I started out about two or three doe rabbits and one buck. Rabbits are fast to multiply, so I soon had quite a number of rabbits. The thing was to sell them. Not everybody had a taste for rabbit meat, but I managed to sell all the rabbits I raised. I got to the point of butchering between 15 and 18 rabbits every Thursday afternoon. I got pretty fast at it and would stretch the hides on wire hide stretchers made especially for that. Every month or so I would send the hides to a tanning company in Missouri. After my brothers left for the Service and I was busy on the farm, I sold the rabbit project and turned the paper route over to another kid.

I loved farming and Dad would always give me a field to raise my own crop on. Since we lived in town and drove five miles out to the farm each day, we would eat lunch at the farm. Lunch time was a special time for me and I hold it dear in my memory. Dad bought an old milk truck van body and we set it out there for a "lunch house". We put two windows in it and a back door. There was just room enough for a "kitchen counter" where we kept the dishes, the canned food, our camp stove and a wash pan. Mulligan Stew, noodle soup or beans. On each side we put a little cot which doubled for chairs and a little table in the middle. We heated the food with the camp stove and washed the dishes immediately after eating. The joy of the whole thing was just talking about the farm, about anything that came up. It was fellowship. I didn't realize it, but Dad was passing on wisdom from his generation to the next. Not only wisdom but values. The values I received like that from my Dad became part and parcel of my life. Those values are hard to jar loose!

The first year I was out of High School, we planted 100 acres of corn, about 70 acres (besides the grain and hay) on our place and 30 on Bill Owen's farm across the road. Back then, the county average was about 45 bushels to the acre and we beat the average. We made 52 bushels! Compared to later yields of 200 bushels or more it wasn't much but for back then, on sandy ground and sparse irrigation and 36 inch rows it was good. That fall Dad and I both worked at the sugar factory. That fit in pretty good with our farming operation because the campaign started about the tenth of October and lasted till about the first of the year. Dad was feeding cattle that year and I picked corn when our shift at the factory was at night. In the factory we worked eight hours, seven days a week and every two weeks switched shifts. Eight to four was the day shift, then midnight till eight in the morning, then four until midnight. When we were on either of the two night shifts I picked corn with a one row picker. During that campaign I finished picking the one hundred acres and stacked it in big a rick. By Christmas time I was really tired. I had just a little left to do after Christmas. There was snow on the ground and it was really cold. That last load was really hard but I could say I finished the job!

Dad sold the corn "ground into their trucks" to neighbors who had a big cattle operation. We filled two truckloads each Saturday. I would shovel the corn into the hopper and Dad would feed it into the grinder. I was eighteen that year.

CHAPTER TWELVE
Walking Out

I really don't remember why, but the next spring we didn't have much farming to do and I felt deep down kind of disoriented and useless. I took some buddies to the swimming pool in Boulder, about 20 miles away. On the way back a rod came loose in the engine and I had to ask Dad to tow me home.

The next day I packed a few clothes in a sack and walked out the door without so much as saying goodbye. I hitch hiked to Brighton, eight miles to the south. My friend Bob Libhart had told me he could get me a job in Kuners Pickle Factory. His future father in law was Foreman there. He hired me as a truck driver. My job would be to deliver pickles to the factory from all the pickle docks strung out along the railroad from Henderson south of Brighton all the way to Ault, north of Greeley, about 50 miles in total. Each day I would be sent to different docks.

After I got the job, I needed a place to stay and someplace to eat. I didn't have any money but there was a very large rooming house near the factory that belonged to the Great Western Sugar Company for farm and factory workers. I talked to the lady that ran the place and she said I could stay there and pay when I got paid. Then I went to Pete's Bar and Grill over on the highway. They were accustomed to giving workers a "meal ticket" for their meals between paydays, so I had no problem with that. But there was a problem in that my work started at six in the morning and the restaurant didn't open till seven. But the cook, "Big Red" (and she was very big, over six feet tall) was an amiable sort and she agreed to come and make my breakfast if I would just wake her up at the cabin camp where she lived. So each morning at five I would be at her door knocking. She would walk with me to the restaurant and fix my breakfast. I don't know what people thought that may have seen us walking together in the mornings, but I wasn't worried about what people thought.

I hadn't said a word to Mom and Dad when I left. It never occurred to me that they might be hurt. Typically of the immature, I was thinking only of myself. I worked sixteen to eighteen hours a day, seven days a week and loved it. I was a big wheel driving a truck loaded with ten and a half tons of pickles! At the Henderson dock I almost lost a load on the steep grade up to the highway. The truck was overloaded and the front end came off the ground. It was a new truck and had good brakes, so the brakes held but there I was with the front wheels off the ground. I eased it back down with sweat pouring down my neck! So I angled up on to the highway, praying that the truck wouldn't tip over sideways! Never thought about unloading the back end enough to make it safe to pull out. My own rule was to take all the pickles they had no matter how big the load was!

My last job each day was to take a load of culls out from the factory to where they dumped them in a pit out east of Brighton. That would be after ten at night and sometimes I had to wait till eleven when they finished the last run of the day. That would be my last trip of the day. I would bring the truck back to the factory, park it there and walked a block to my rooming house. Sleeping was no problem, but I would be up again at 4:45. The factory never shuts down until the "campaign" is over. Once they heat the boilers up, the process has to continue until they shut down for the season. I loved it though. I had gotten disgusted with myself for not working and then when I knocked a rod out of my car, I decided to change. Now I felt better about myself. Meanwhile, I was planning in my head how I would rebuild my car engine and "hop it up" (built for racing).

One of the pickle docks was at Fort Lupton, my home town. I was there to pick up a load and the foreman asked me to first take out their culls. I had never communicated with my family, though I had been working for more than a month. The way to the dump took me past our house, so I stopped in to say hello. Mom said, "<u>Where have you</u> <u>been?</u>" I said, "In Brighton, Why?" As if it was a funny question for her to ask! After the pickle season I did a month tour in the Marine Corps Reserve, including some time in California which will be part of another story.

In August I came back home and helped Dad finish up the crops and that fall we both again worked in the Sugar Factory. Before the sugar campaign was over, however, I left for the Service. I left Dad alone on the farm, but I had pretty much done that all that year. Looking back now as a father and Christian, I think my folks might have been deeply hurt by my attitude and lack of communication, though they never said as much. The three older boys including me now had left the farm. Then dry years and poor prices finally forced Dad out. He made a comeback though as a builder, developing a new neighborhood, providing good homes for middle income families at good prices. After military service I learned the building trade from him. Getting married and starting a family brought changes in my life of course, but God also had other plans for me that I would have never even dreamed of. But that would make another story........!

The Plowman